S Beside You

*Heavenly Lessons
on Living Life and Transcending Grief*

Patricia Overton
&
Raymond Overton

outskirts
press

Still Beside You
Heavenly Lessons on Living Life and Transcending Grief
All Rights Reserved.
Copyright © 2022 Patricia Overton and Raymond Overton
v3.0

The opinions expressed in this manuscript are solely the opinions of the author and do not represent the opinions or thoughts of the publisher. The author has represented and warranted full ownership and/or legal right to publish all the materials in this book.

This book may not be reproduced, transmitted, or stored in whole or in part by any means, including graphic, electronic, or mechanical without the express written consent of the publisher except in the case of brief quotations embodied in critical articles and reviews.

Outskirts Press, Inc.
http://www.outskirtspress.com

ISBN: 978-1-9772-3810-8

Cover Photo © 2022 www.gettyimages.com. All rights reserved - used with permission.

Outskirts Press and the "OP" logo are trademarks belonging to Outskirts Press, Inc.

PRINTED IN THE UNITED STATES OF AMERICA

To Mom, Dad, Grandma Rawson
and her children
*Thank you for encouraging
my spirit to fly!*

Table of Contents

Chapter One: The Beginning of the End 1
Chapter Two: The Journey Begins 5
Chapter Three: Expanded Consciousness 12
Chapter Four: Moving On 18
Chapter Five: Connection 22
Chapter Six: A Voice in the Darkness 25
Chapter Seven: Enhanced Communication 36
Chapter Eight: Turning Point 40
Chapter Nine: Coming to Terms 48
Chapter Ten: Patrick Mathews 72
Chapter Eleven: Changing Perception 80
Chapter Twelve: A New Adventure 92
Chapter Thirteen: Stepping Outside the Box 96
Chapter Fourteen: Forging Ahead 101
Chapter Fifteen: Finding Joy 108
Chapter Sixteen: Acclimation 122
Chapter Seventeen: Checking In 128
Chapter Eighteen: Full Circle 136

Chapter One

The Beginning of the End

That first morning was like no other. I hope I never experience anything like it again. As I cracked open my eyes and waded into consciousness, the usual feelings of joy, hope and excitement for a new day, surrounded by the people I love, were instantly shattered and replaced with the crushing weight of darkness, physical pain and despair. It truly felt as though someone had cut a hole in my heart. I lost half my soul. A vault had slammed shut. My life would never be the same. What would I do now…or should I even care?

Six days ago our family was going about its normal routine. It was the end of Christmas holiday break, a Sunday. Ray was working outside, running up to the house with a wheelbarrow full of firewood, as I watched out the sliding doors. My daughter and I were teachers. I was doing house chores and both of us were completing school work. We were preparing for the week ahead.

That night, as Ray and I watched television upstairs, Ray exercised on the NordicTrack. Suddenly, totally unlike him, he halted abruptly and darted downstairs. Confused and concerned, I trailed after him. When I arrived in the kitchen, he was quietly tying up a garbage bag to take outdoors. I interrupted and asked why he left upstairs so suddenly. He sputtered that he had a pain in his chest, but pointed to the joint in his shoulder where, intermittently, he'd had pain since his twenties. Again, confused and now alarmed, I blurted, "What??? A pain in your chest??"

He softly, quickly, and reassuringly interjected, "NO, NO, Pat, it's nothing! It's just a pulled ligament!"

I scanned his face and body looking for any little thing that might tell me he was wrong. I could find nothing – no shortness of breath, sweating, redness in the face, no clutching of the chest. He was moving very normally, peacefully – rhythmically tying the bag and talking to me while looking reassuringly into my eyes. I shook my head slowly and said, "Ray, I don't know. This doesn't sound right." Very deliberately and firmly, in no apparent pain he reiterated, "Pat, trust me, it's just a pulled ligament."

Using the word ligament was not a typical word in Ray's vocabulary. I could only think a doctor had labeled this pain as such during a routine physical exam. He had two physicals a year by two different types of doctors – a naturopathic doctor and a traditional medical doctor, not because he had anything "wrong" with him, but because his father had passed from a heart attack and Ray didn't want to experience the same fate. He had just undergone a physical last month. Both doctors had reassured him he was in the peak of health – absolutely no health issues. I had looked at Ray's blood work results. Everything was right where it should be. So, I looked at him and with some hesitation replied "Alright, Ray, but tomorrow morning, we're going to the doctor." He turned to go outside, shrugged his shoulders and said "OK".

That was the last time I saw him conscious. I'd returned upstairs to watch television when I heard what sounded like someone laying down something soft on the kitchen floor – a garbage bag? I waited to hear the door latch. Not a sound. I ran downstairs and found him lying on the floor in the entry way. His eyes were closed, his breath barely audible, but raspy.

My mind raced, trying to grasp what I was seeing in front of me. What should I do? CPR…I started to try, then quickly realized I couldn't remember exactly how to do it…Begged for the angels to help…Called 911.

I gave my name and address and what was happening. They made me repeat! There was no time! They tried to instruct me on how to do CPR over the phone while I was trying to cradle the receiver between my neck and shoulder. We were progressing, but time was racing. They asked if anyone else was home – to run and get them. I thought I heard my daughter outdoors. I immediately opened the front door and yelled for her. Not there.

The Beginning of the End

Ran to the stairs inside the house. Screamed upstairs. She was down the stairs and on the floor giving CPR in an instant. She was amazing! Within five minutes the ambulance arrived. The EMTs pulled Ray into the next room, cut off his jacket and did a tracheotomy on the floor. He was breathing! They carried him into the ambulance.

I was in my P.J.'s – no shoes, socks, there was snow on the ground outside. I didn't want them to take him away without me. I ran through the snow in my bare feet and climbed into the ambulance. I asked if I could sit in the back of the ambulance with him and give him Reiki en route to the hospital. They said no. I needed to sit in front. I jumped into the front seat, but was feeling lightheaded. I was going to faint. I needed a paper bag. I asked the driver and he handed me a bag. I lowered my head and started to breathe. We were off to the hospital, but not the one I wanted. I was told that another was closer.

It was winter. It was cold, foggy and damp. We were proceeding carefully through the fog to the hospital. We lost Ray three times. Each time I yelled, "Ray, get back here!" He returned.

Within fifteen minutes, we reached the ER. Ray was stabilized and they wanted to take him by Life Star to the city hospital, but it was too foggy. So…we traveled by ambulance. It was a one-half hour trip. I was sitting in the front seat of the ambulance giving Ray Reiki the entire time.

Once at the hospital, they wheeled him in for surgery. He survived. He was now taken to the ICU and we would wait for signs of consciousness. At one point in the next five days, a nurse tried to clean his teeth and he grimaced. We were ecstatic, but the medical community told us that this was not what they needed to see. Why? No explanation given. His feet moved, but again we were told – not what was needed. What did they want? What did they need? There were no answers forthcoming. Groups of doctors walked by our glassed in room. They paused and conferenced. They glanced into the room. No one talked to us and they moved on. On day five in the hospital, we were brought to a meeting where we were told that Ray suffered a blow to the head. Head injury??? How??? They replied that there was no head injury, but lack of oxygen to the brain. At the time of the incident he apparently had a clogged carotid artery and now there was no brain activity. Tests were scheduled with approximately twelve of us present to prove and witness that he could not survive on his own. There was absolutely no doubt at the completion of the tests. With our family surrounding him, any life support was removed the next day.

Chapter Two
The Journey Begins

Ray and I met while I was in college. We were married in our early twenties. He was in construction, then taught for a while. I was a language teacher. Not making very much money back then, we weren't sure we would be able to afford a house. Both of us had difficulty finding jobs when we finished school, but Ray had worked for a short time with his cousin who was a highly regarded builder in town. Ray always wanted to build his own home, so we did. It took nine months with frequent assistance from his students and some family members, working every night after work. Weekends, we worked on the house together. When completed, it was small. It looked a lot like a one room school house, but it was our Taj Mahal. It was an absolute labor of love that took us six years in the making – saving money, purchasing land and building. Two years later our daughter was born into a close knit extended family of grandparents, great aunts and uncles, aunts, uncles and cousins. We became active in our local church. Life was good.

As time passed and family members grew older and transitioned – some to colleges, some to other parts of the country, others succumbing to illnesses and crossing over, our cocoon eroded. One elderly aunt who had been living out West, decided to move back East. She was single. Liz, Ray and I went out to help. While we were helping pack her apartment, I came across a book by renowned psychic medium Sylvia Browne. Prior to this encounter, I'm not sure how I felt about mediums – definitely skeptical but my aunt, who was a *very* skeptical person, was very impressed by her and introduced me to her autobiography. Therein began a metaphysical journey that had actually been sparked when I was in high school but ignited now, and it caught Ray's attention as well.

We attended a few of Sylvia's lectures over the course of the next few years. One day, while I was watching a talk show, Sylvia Browne happened to be the guest. She gave a short gallery reading for the audience and then began to talk about heaven and what happens when our loved ones cross over. One person in the audience raised her hand and said something like, 'Sylvia, you are able to see and communicate with deceased loved ones, but we can't.'

Sylvia interrupted, shook her head and replied (to the best of my recollection), 'everyone has the ability to do this. It's just that some people are more gifted than others.' She went on to say that our deceased loved ones are right here with us, just a few feet from us on a different plane, and all we have to do is ask for them to connect with us and they will! 'In fact,' she continued, 'all you have to do is to take a piece of paper and write, Dear _____, would you please pay me a visit, sign your name and place it somewhere the note can lie undisturbed. Then let your deceased loved ones decide the when, where and how it will happen.'

For the next few days, after watching the program, I replayed her words over and over in my head. 'Anyone can connect with their loved ones on the Other Side. All you have to do is ask.' So, I decided to give this a try. I found a sheet of paper and on it I wrote:

Dear Daddy, Uncle Irv, Uncle Charles and Aunt Jean,
    I miss you SO much and would love to have you pay me a visit around Christmas. But please know that you're going to have to bang me over the head with whatever sign you give me, because I'm stupid and I'm not going to believe it's you!
    Love, Pat

Sylvia, of course, had instructed us *not* to say "when" we wanted our loved ones to visit, but I tossed that in anyway. Then, having written the message, I placed the note on my bureau in our bedroom, under my trinket box. It was summer now, and I would wait to see what, if anything happened.

I actually forgot about that note. Late summer and fall came. No obvious signs from the Other Side crossed my path. We entered November, December and finally Christmas Eve arrived. Christmas Eve, my daughter, husband and I were sitting in our loft, eating dinner and watching "A Christmas Carol" in the stillness of the night. Most of the lights in the house were off, except for the artificial candles lit in the windows, the Christmas tree lights and some candles in the living room downstairs. All of a sudden, we were startled by a very unusual…THUMP, downstairs!!

All three of us quickly turned our heads and stared at each other. What the heck was that? Ray and I peered over the loft railing, looking downstairs into the living room, holding our breath and listening, but nothing. We glanced at each other. I turned to Ray and said, "You take the basement. I'll take the first floor." He gingerly walked down the stairs into the basement. I cautiously examined the first floor. Nothing. So, I walked back upstairs. Ray followed, but as he strolled by the Christmas tree in the living room, he noticed an ornament on the floor, in the corner by the stairs.

He yelled up, "An ornament fell off the tree!"
"An ornament fell off the tree?" I replied.
"…Yeah"
"Which one?"
"…The glass ball."
"Did it break?"
"No….."
"…What happened? Was it not pushed in far enough? Did the string loop break?"
"No…the loop is still attached and intact."
"……….NOTHING is broken??"

I was dumbfounded. We both were.

Ray slowly picked up the glass ornament and placed it back on the tree. He drifted up the stairs and sat down on the couch. We restarted the movie, but continued to be a little puzzled. Ornaments didn't just fall off trees and this was a blue spruce. The tree was too dense and the needles were way too thick! The ornament string had to be jumped up and over the needles to even place the ornament on the tree. We never had an ornament fall off a tree before except when the cat used to knock them off and then we used to purposely place the ornaments loosely on the bottom branches specifically for the cat. Now, we had no cat. The dog was with us, upstairs. There was no earthquake. There were no small children. This seemed crazy. Oh well, we went back to eating.

About an hour later, still watching the movie, we heard a loud……THUD, downstairs. We all turned our heads again and stared at each other. Now what? Both Ray and I got up slowly, looked over the loft railing and saw nothing. Ray went downstairs and surveyed the basement while I toured the first floor. We met at the top of the basement stairs finding nothing amiss. I continued upstairs to the loft. Ray lagged behind, but as he rounded the corner to climb the stairs he paused and said, "Another ornament fell off the tree."

"…Which one?" I asked.

"The wooden nutcracker," he replied.

"Did it break?"

"No," he said.

"Did the attachment loop break?"

"No, it's still on," he responded hesitantly. He placed the ornament back on the tree. He climbed the stairs, slowly - thinking - and sat next to me on the couch once more. We were both quiet – silently brainstorming – trying to figure out what just happened. The movie continued to play. Then, after a few minutes, Ray turned to me and said with a smile, "Aunt Jean?"

Surprised at what he just suggested I replied, "I don't know…..Do you think so?" Then, it hit me. "Ray," I began. "I wrote a note and left it on my bureau."

I told him the entire story of how I had watched Sylvia Browne on television and how she told the audience they could connect with their deceased loved ones just by asking. He stared at me and said, "Do you think that's what's happening now? Do you think it could be real?"

Pausing, I replied, "I don't know. Do YOU think it could be real?"

He just sat there with his mouth partially open and slowly and softly whispered, "I don't know."

We continued to half watch TV, wondering if there might be anything to this or not – people from the Other Side communicating with us by dropping ornaments off our Christmas tree! Honestly, in our hearts, this seemed to make some sort of perfect sense, but our heads were getting in the way.

The next day, after Christmas dinner at my sister's house, we left for Florida. We returned five days later, on a Sunday. The following day we returned to work. Immediately after school, I was off to have my hair cut. I arrived home around 5:00 pm. It was dark. Liz had been home alone. As I pulled into the driveway, I noticed she was standing in the front entrance to the house with the door wide open, staring at me as I drove in. As soon as I opened the car door, she nervously said, "Mom…"

I replied, "What, what's the matter, are you OK?"

She continued, "Mom…..something weird just happened."

"What, what happened?" I asked.

"Well, I was in the kitchen. I was going to try to start dinner. The lights were off in the house except where I was working. I was thinking about Aunt Jean and wondering if people really can communicate with their dead relatives, when my thoughts were interrupted with a big THUD. I was really scared because it was dark and I was all by myself. I wanted to run, but I turned on the lights and went into the living room. My porcelain angel that was on the Christmas tree was now on the floor, three feet from the tree." I asked if the ornament was broken.

Shaking her head slowly in disbelief she murmured- "No."

Then we stared at each other, eyes locked, giggled and decided that if

Aunt Jean was doing this (assuming she was ultimately responsible for all three incidences – even though I had written to four people) she would have to start picking on objects other than glass or china ornaments. We laughed and went on to other things.

A few days later, I came home after school to an empty house (except for our miniature schnauzer). Liz was visiting a friend. I laid down my bags on the kitchen table, picked up the dog, per routine, and took her outdoors. I then reentered the house, carrying the dog in my arms and climbed over the gate that separated the dog in the kitchen from the rest of the house during the day. As I walked into the living room, I noticed that our Christmas tree bird's nest, typically cradled in the branches in the top *back* half of the tree, near the trunk, was out on the wooden floor about three feet in *front* of the tree. Dumbfounded, my first thought regarding what I was seeing was, 'could the dog have done this?' My next thought was 'of course not!' The tree is seven feet tall. The nest was tucked inside the tree about five and a half feet from the ground. The dog is a miniature schnauzer. She couldn't jump that high and, even if she could, the dog was penned in the kitchen. She couldn't even jump the kitchen gate. On top of that, the nest had been in the *back* of the tree, but was now on the floor, three feet in *front* of the tree. If, for some crazy reason, the nest had fallen from its original location, it would have either ended up caught in the branches below, or it would have fallen *behind* or *next to* the tree, but would not have traveled 180 degrees to the front of the tree and landed three feet in front of it! Finding it very difficult to believe what I was seeing, I just stared at the nest on the floor. That was the fourth and last of the ornament events. We took our tree down a little over a month later.

A week or so after that last incident, I called my Aunt Joyce, my mom and Aunt Jean's sister, who lived in Arizona. I told her the entire Christmas tree story. Without hesitation, she jumped in when I finished, and commented that she totally believed that all of this was communication from the Other Side, and she could tell me exactly which person was responsible for each of the falling ornaments. According to Aunt Joyce, the glass ball

The Journey Begins

ornament would have been her brother, my Uncle Charles. They used to go Christmas shopping together and he was always intrigued with hand blown glass balls. The nutcracker would have been her brother, Irv. He loved fantasy stories like "The March of the Wooden Soldiers" and "The Nutcracker." The angel would have been my dad. Aunt Joyce said that she, my mom and dad loved to go into the stores at Christmas. He was fascinated by angels. Then, the nest would have been Aunt Jean. She was a nature lover who loved to take her younger siblings, nephews and my brother, sister and I on nature walks in the woods by her house.

During the entire time my husband and I were married, we always had a Christmas tree. Ornaments **never** "fell off" our tree except during the few years we had a cat. As mentioned previously, we used to deliberately place ornaments at the bottom of the tree so he could entertain himself by batting the ornaments and knocking them off the tree. The only other time an ornament ever fell off the tree was about eight years after the first Christmas tree incidents described above. I was working in the spare room – computer room, upstairs. It was a few weeks after Christmas and I was thinking about my dad. Out loud I said, "Dad, I really miss you. I sure wish I could hear from you."

Within an hour, downstairs, a candy cane dropped off our Christmas tree.

Chapter Three
Expanded Consciousness

Sylvia Browne and that Christmas "miracle" initiated a very focused, dynamic spiritual journey for Ray and me and the Universe seemed ready and eager to embrace us. As questions arose, in regard to different facets of our being – who we really were, why we were here, what we were actually capable of, what happened when we died, etc., the Universe opened up and provided us with answers and resources to give us a fuller, broader perspective of our existence.

What began with Sylvia Browne, now continued with Reiki. I was sitting in a salon chair one day, having my hair cut when Bill, the owner/stylist, began talking about his brother. Apparently this brother had pulled into Bill's driveway at home quite unexpectedly. When Bill went out to greet him and asked how he was, his brother shared that he'd been in the hospital in Boston with a brain infection – toxoplasmosis. While in the hospital, a volunteer had come into his room and offered him Reiki. I asked what that was. Bill replied he wasn't sure. He offered only that his brother, who was *not* into any kind of alternative "medicine," was very impressed with the treatment. Since Bill couldn't provide me with any more information about this "Reiki," I decided to just file what little information I had in the back of my brain. If I ever went to the hospital and was asked if I wanted Reiki, since it sounded as though it could possibly be very beneficial, I would say, "Yes."

About three weeks later, I received a catalog in the mail advertising adult education classes in the northeast corner of the state. I opened the catalog and my eyes fell on one of the first classes listed, "Reiki." The description read something like this: 'Would you like to know more about Reiki? Reiki is a non-invasive ancient Japanese healing technique being used in hospitals and convalescent homes all over the United States.'

I thought, "What a crazy coincidence!" The class was a two hour informational session and cost $25. I definitely wanted to go but was a little hesitant. The class was at night in a very quiet, unfamiliar corner of the state. I asked Ray if there was any chance he might be willing to drive me there, drop me off and go for coffee. Much to my surprise, he said he'd be happy to drive and would like to go to the class. "Wow!" I thought. This was fantastic!

A few weeks later, off we went. Our teacher reiterated a bit of what she had written in the class description. She spoke a little about the eastern origins of Reiki. She then instructed us to position our hands so that our palms faced each other in front of us, and then asked if we felt any pressure or anything between our hands. All six of us said, "No." She then asked us to sit up straight in our folding chairs, which were arranged in a circle and to close our eyes. We were asked to follow her in a loving meditation. She then asked us to remain with our eyes closed and just relax. Peaceful music played in the background. She was going to place her hands on our shoulders and we might feel warmth.

I was very skeptical. Were we being hypnotized? But she didn't speak. There was no "suggestion" offered. Just silence. When she came to me and laid her hands on my shoulders for about five minutes, her hands felt very warm. After she placed her hands on everyone, she told us we could open our eyes. She then asked us to reposition our hands so that the palms faced each other and asked if we felt any energy or pressure between our hands. Surprised, most of us replied, "Yes, we could!" She subsequently spoke a little about classes she was giving and we left.

What just happened? While Ray and I were driving home, I asked him what he thought about this Reiki and what he thought it was. He replied, "I don't know. What did *you* think? Could *you* figure out what it was?"

I answered, "No." I asked if he felt anything when the teacher laid her hands on his shoulders. He explained that her hands were very warm and that he felt as though something was being drawn from him. Then, with some hesitation, he relayed that in his mind's eye he'd had a vision of all of our relatives who had passed recently, walking toward him. He truly believed they wanted to tell him something, but just as one of them was about to speak, an outside noise startled him, and he lost the vision. He was very disappointed. He'd **never** had an experience like that before. Then he was quiet and very pensive. We both just sat and thought.

There was no doubt in my mind that something unusual had happened. I definitely believed he'd had that vision. Ray then asked if *I* noticed anything in particular when the teacher laid her hands on *my* shoulders. I told him that her hands were very warm, and it felt really soothing, but nothing else. We continued our ride in silence, trying to navigate our way through this new experience.

It was around 10:00 pm when we arrived home – an hour past our school night bedtime. We would need to hurry to bed in order to get enough sleep for work tomorrow. As I was getting ready, I noticed something. That night, right before attending the Reiki class, I was very tired. My stomach hurt. I had an intestinal infection, and my naturopath told me that if I wanted to get to the root of this issue, I was going to have to follow some strict dietary restrictions, along with her prescribed remedies to treat the situation. In short, she said I'd be in pain for several months until the issue began to clear. I had been in pain every day for about two months. I was in pain before the class. Now, however, the pain was completely gone. I felt absolutely nothing AND I wasn't tired! Since I hadn't done anything except go to the Reiki class, I could only surmise it must have been whatever the instructor had done that helped me.

I called upstairs to Ray, told him what happened and asked if he would be interested in taking a class. He paused, hesitant in large part because of the cost. Then I said to him, "But look what it might have done. Think about how much we pay in co-pays. This isn't a substitute for conventional medicine, but if it could help us in any way – to ease some pain and/or help us heal faster as the instructor mentioned, wouldn't it be worth it? Wouldn't this be a valuable tool in our health toolbox?" He decided that when you looked at the cost through that lens, the cost was really negligible.

So, we took that first Reiki class and eventually became Reiki masters three times over. With Reiki we learned to sense energy and energy shifts around ourselves and others. In addition, we learned that when we used Reiki, not only could it help with physical and emotional issues – large and small, for ourselves and others, but when practiced routinely, it could help to expand consciousness as well.

Ray and I used to give ourselves a Reiki "treatment" for one half hour each day after dinner. One evening, about two months into our practice, as I was lying down with eyes closed, giving myself Reiki, something unusual happened. In my mind's eye, as clear as if I was watching a movie on a TV screen, I found myself standing in the woods, at the bottom of a hill. I was observing people dressed in what seemed to be 17th century clothing, standing near a period-appropriate carriage, which had stopped in the middle of a dirt road. It was my understanding that there was a king and/or queen either *inside* or *behind* the carriage. Somehow I felt I was definitely a part of the entourage, waiting to be instructed as to what to do. I was not a member of the royal family. I could not see any part of myself. It was as if I was a fly on the wall.

Several years later, I had an angel reading by one of *Angelspeake's* authors, Trudy Griswold. She knew nothing at all about me at the time of the reading. She had no knowledge of this aforementioned experience. She told me during the reading, however, that in a past life I had been a Sherpa who used to lead a king across the mountains. Did this explain what I had seen in my "vision"? It felt plausible.

Both Ray and I also began to experience connections to the Other Side with a frequency we had never felt before. We would walk into a room in our house and smell baby powder, (something no one in the family used), later to be verified by my mother as a scent attributed to her deceased mother, my grandmother. Ray and I both woke up on several occasions at different times smelling smoke that, by memory, belonged to cigarettes or cigars smoked by my deceased father or my uncle.

One night I was awakened by a very strange odor. As I lay in bed with my eyes closed, I began to smell what seemed like urine on cedar shavings. How did I recognize that smell? Ray and I had a guinea pig when we were first married, and his cage was lined with cedar shavings. So this smell was in our memory bank. The instant I realized what the smell was, the thought of my brother's first wife came to mind. She had passed tragically, very young, years ago from a longstanding heart condition. I began to cry so deeply that I had to get out of bed and go into the bathroom for fear of waking my husband. While I was sobbing, half awake and trying to hold onto the small remainder of my sleep state, I was also trying to figure out what was happening and why this smell was coming to me. I was also not a person who would cry at the drop of a hat, and here I was sobbing uncontrollably, not totally understanding why. My brother had remarried years ago. I hadn't thought of his first wife in ages. Then, in the next few minutes, this overwhelming feeling came that I was supposed to tell my brother, "it is OK – not to be upset" and it all had something to do with this situation.

A few weeks passed, and I happened to be speaking to my brother on the phone. When a lull in the conversation occurred, I said, "Joe, did you and Lorraine ever have a guinea pig?" He said, "No, why?"

I said, "Because I know this is going to sound really crazy, but a few weeks ago, I was awakened in the middle of the night by the smell of urine on cedar shavings. We had a guinea pig and that smell was part of the guinea pig experience. But I also started thinking of Lorraine at the same time, and so I thought it maybe had something to do with you and Lorraine – that you had a guinea pig."

For about five seconds there was dead silence. Then Joe began, "Pat, I never told anyone this, but right before Lorraine died, we had gone into a pet shop. She saw this little dog and really wanted it, but I told her no. I didn't think it was a good idea. I was carrying her up and down the stairs." (She was very ill at the time – very weak.) "I didn't feel that we could take care of a dog the way we should. Well, Lorraine passed and not too long after, I don't know why I did this, but I went back to the pet store. I felt so badly that I didn't buy it for her when she wanted it. The dog was still there, and I bought the dog. The dog had been trained to go on cedar shavings, so I bought cedar shavings to use in the training at home. I was grieving. The dog was too much for me to handle at that time, and while I felt terrible, I decided to take the dog back. I took the dog back to the shop and told the owner I didn't need any money back. I just wanted him to find a good home for the dog."

I paused for a few seconds and then said, "Joe, I really think Lorraine wanted me to tell you that she knows what you did and she thanks you so much for trying. She understands everything, loves you for it and it's all OK."

As the years passed, Ray and I continued to be tugged by a curiosity to understand the truth of the spiritual world we lived in. As such, we were led to explore other disciplines. While we had been brought up Christian and sought to understand its different branches, we now took a look at other religions, as well, including Buddhism. In addition we studied and/or took classes on meditation, indigenous energy healing, crystals and crystal healing, intuitive communication, angels, nature spirits and tree whispering. What was real, when it came to spiritual truths and what was not? We needed to try to find out for ourselves. We were stunned by what we found.

One of the most important discoveries, in regard to those latter disciplines, was the importance of "breath." Our breath, it seemed, could not only help us to invigorate, relax and heal, but help us to connect with ourselves, others and the rest of the universe. While we may have thought that all beings were separate entities, we began to realize that maybe we were not. Maybe there was something to the idea that we were all one.

Chapter Four

Moving On

We all know that life is transient and most of us don't want to live forever. We know that we will not be with our loved ones forever on this earthly plane. When we marry or are in a long term devoted partnership, we know that one partner will probably pass before the other. And yet, when our loved ones pass, depending on the type and depth of our relationship and/or the strength of that love bond, we can be devastated. And so, coupled with the complete surprise of Ray's passing, I was in total shock.

Could I function? Did I get out of bed in the morning, get dressed, work, etc.? Yes, I did, although I know there are some people who simply cannot. I was amazed, however, that for a person who, all my life, loved to eat, that I did not feel hungry at all. It fascinated me that I could go all day without eating and neither my brain nor my stomach would tell me I needed to do otherwise. Thank goodness for the kindness, support and perseverance of friends and some family members who tried to look after me. I knew I needed to care about work and home, including bills, upkeep, firewood for the stove, snow removal, the lawyer and all the myriad number of things to do when settling "an estate" (that somehow you felt you really shouldn't be asked to do at a time like this). But otherwise, as far as the rest was concerned, the overriding feeling was, "I don't care." I couldn't care. I was too overwhelmed. I had just been blind-sided.

My daughter visited a grief counselor. She suggested I do the same. Some people tried to comfort any way they knew how, for months (thank goodness) and more, which was so thoughtful and kind of them. There are still no words to express my gratitude. Other people stayed away, probably not understanding what they could do. After all, as a society we don't really talk very much about "handling" grief. Perhaps they didn't understand that a phone call or a meal, a hug, a thinking of you card or text, an emoji, a little quip, any kind of connection/communication with loving intent, no matter how small, could be sincerely treasured.

I went to see a grief counselor. She was a good listener. In some ways the sessions were helpful. Once a week you knew you had someone with whom you could completely let down your guard and cry as much as you wanted, with no judgment. I also took away a few thoughts which definitely assisted me at the time, and which I have shared with others going through something similar. She told me that as I went through the grief process, that people would look at me and, seeing that I physically appeared essentially the same as before, would treat me as before and expect the same from me, not realizing I was a paraplegic inside. She added that scientists have now determined that the brain physiologically shuts down during grief as in a concussion. I remembered thinking –"Oh, so is that the reason for the blank look so many people have while in the grief state?" She also commented that it normally takes three to five years to work your way through your loss with many waves of ups and downs. Of course, there are those who need more time.

Going to counseling was helpful, but it didn't begin to touch the sadness I felt. I remember telling a friend once that I had always been a person who woke up in the morning with a smile, ready for the excitement of a new day and new possibilities. I always believed light would extinguish darkness. I never knew how deep and dark depression could be. Could I function? Absolutely, but many times at night or when I was alone, I felt like I was trapped in this black pit and I didn't know how to get out – how I could ever get out.

I never thought that "joy" could be attached to such a great extent to the people with whom I did things. It wasn't so much eating the piece of chocolate cake that gave me joy as with whom I was eating the chocolate cake.

Now, how would I turn this around?

I was trying counseling. I was trying various meditations. I was too overwhelmed, as some suggested, to try new "adventures." Just surviving and coping with all the day to day events and situations on my own were "adventures" enough. Everything, and there were hundreds of things it seemed, needed to be relearned, including who I was without Ray. I wanted and needed to see people, but I could only keep myself "up" for about an hour. After that, it was too much of a struggle. Ray and I had done so much together that it was difficult to do much of anything that didn't bring up memories of him, and memories were painful. They reminded me that he wasn't there.

Then I remembered that when my uncle died, my daughter, who was very close to him, had read a book that she really felt came to her rescue. It was a book by a New York Times bestselling author and medium named Patrick Mathews. She had asked me, at the time, if I wanted to read the book. I'd read a couple of other books in a similar vein, so I declined. Now, though, in my effort to find answers, I asked if she still had the book and if I might borrow and read it. Happy to oblige, she retrieved the book and I devoured it. It was **exactly** what I needed to hear –*Never Say Goodbye*. Even though there was a part of me that had been introduced to most of the information presented from other sources – that our souls survive "death" and live on (Christmas Eve with Aunt Jean, Uncle Irv, Uncle Charles and Dad), it was great to hear this truth again. Our loved ones still existed and we **could** connect with them. All was not over. But I connected with my father, aunt and uncles once in ten years. Was it possible for me to do this with Ray and would/could it be enough? There were serious doubts on both counts.

Many years ago, I don't exactly remember when, I once watched the medium James Van Praagh on television giving a reading before a large audience. I don't remember all the details of what transpired, but I remember the essence of the story. He was giving a gallery reading and communicated that he was connecting with a deceased woman, whose first name he gave as well as how she passed. He then declared that she had a female family member in the audience, whose name began with a letter he voiced. He asked if anyone resonated with this information. Several people raised their hands and stood. James expressed that this deceased woman wanted to thank her family member for going to her gravesite each week and placing her favorite flower (an unusual flower, which he named) on her grave. He asked if any one of the people standing resonated with this. One woman gasped and said, 'I never told anyone this – including my husband, but I go every week before work to place those flowers (named) on her grave.' James added, 'She knows. She can see you and she thanks you.' I remember being astounded.

He then told a story about a female client who used to write to a deceased loved one on a regular basis in a journal. One day, during a reading with him, this deceased loved one came through to James' aforementioned client telling her something only *she* would know that she wrote. The deceased loved one wanted to thank her relative for communicating. James told the audience that your loved ones on the Other Side can see you, know what you're doing and if you write to them, they will receive your messages.

I remembered being in awe by that information then, thinking, how could this be? If it was true, it was amazing! So, remembering this again, now, I thought what do I have to lose? If I wrote to Ray, at a minimum, it could give me some peace. If James was right, then Ray would hear me. After all, Aunt Jean, Uncle Charles, Uncle Irv and my dad heard me.

Chapter Five

Connection

January 4th, Ray was brought to the hospital. January 9th, he was taken off life support. January 15th, we held his funeral. January 22nd, after signing some papers at his workplace, I drove into the driveway of our house feeling physically and emotionally spent. Parking the car in the garage, I unfastened my seat belt, leaned over to lie down on the seat next to mine and began to cry. Driving into the yard, my eyes had caught sight of the three towering evergreen trees standing on the side of our property. My mind flashed back to when I was a child, living with my parents. We were fortunate that our house bordered a large expanse of woods. I loved the woods – the spirit, the peace, the tranquility it offered. I loved the trees. They were my friends, my confidants, my playmates. They always made me feel very protected and safe, as if they were watching out for me. I used to go for long walks in those woods or play in the woods with my best friend, Paula. Putting our imaginations together, we built tree houses from fallen trees in my backyard. They were truly joyful days. As a teen, my dad bought some property in a nearby town. The parcel was a wide open field surrounded by stone walls and forest. In the back of the property was this huge evergreen tree. We would go with my dad to the property when he mowed the field with his tractor. While I was waiting for him, I used to love to sit under that tree in my "cave" – my womb, with my back up against the trunk and just soak in the peace, love, joy, security and sheer contentment that both my human family and the trees offered me.

With Ray "gone"--feeling alone and feeling the weight of all I needed to shoulder on my own now--I needed those warm feelings desperately. I took a deep breath, climbed out of the car, walked into the house and changed my clothes. Then, selecting the largest of the evergreens in the side yard, I nestled myself under the branches, placing my back next to the trunk, settling myself on top of the soft bed of fallen needles that covered the snow. As the tree cradled me, I asked the tree for some of its wisdom. Sputtering, I told the tree that Ray had passed and I didn't understand why he had to leave. I took three deep breaths hoping to connect us, and in my head heard the tree say:

All things come from God.
And since we are all from God,
And are all part of God's energy,
We are all one and so cannot ever separate
WE ARE ALL ONE.

I didn't breathe for a second. I was dumbfounded. These were **definitely not** my words. These words did *not* come from *me*. Even though I had asked the tree for a message, I don't know that I actually expected to hear one – like this. I knew I needed to write it down. Back then, I always carried a pen and piece of scrap paper in my coat pocket. I quickly scribbled the message. What the tree spoke resonated with me. It made sense. Perhaps there was a glimmer of hope. Maybe all was not lost. Perhaps Ray, Liz and I were still connected after all, in some way. Please let that be true!

As anyone who has gone through the loss of a dear loved one knows, those early days and months in the aftermath, can be full of pain, darkness and tears. It was no different for me, but even if I felt as though I didn't care about much of anything anymore, my higher self – my subconscious self— wanted me to survive, and so it was determined I would, but how?

I needed to see Ray. I needed to hug him – to connect with him. Over the years I had learned that there were indeed a number of ways our deceased loved ones might/could connect with us. They could use lights or electrical items, for example – turning them on and/or off to communicate their presence. They could connect via dream visitations. I had learned that there were differences between regular dreams that included deceased loved ones and dream visitations. While a regular dream might be illogical or even bizarre – you might be riding a donkey with a deceased uncle and the donkey takes flight. In a true visitation, things would seem very normal and you would likely remember details for a long period of time.

Approximately one week after the tree incident, I was talking to Ray out loud before climbing into bed, telling him how I missed him and wanted to be with him. Before waking the next morning, I dreamt that I saw him, standing all by himself, in what appeared to be the lobby of a grand old theater. He was dressed in jeans, a wool crew neck sweater and an oxford button down shirt. He was facing my daughter and me as we walked toward him. I was not consciously registering at all that he had "died." The three of us wrapped our arms around each other, holding each other in a group embrace. No words were spoken except for my saying, "Ray" and even that may have been telepathically. His smile stood out as did the warmth of his body and the softness of his sweater. I was given just enough time to fully integrate these sensations, and then I awoke.

Instantly, upon regaining consciousness, I *knew* I had been with him. He felt alive. And I'm not sure exactly how to describe it, but all his beautiful essence was there. I was ecstatic!

I knew now that my vehicle for survival had to be connecting with him. But how? It seemed like writing in a journal would be the easiest way to begin. So, I decided I would write to Ray each night, and I never could have imagined what I received.

Chapter Six
A Voice in the Darkness

In the nights following Ray's passing, my daughter and I shared sleeping quarters in our spare room. For an hour or so before slipping under the covers, we'd turn the main lights off and read by the light of one small lamp. This particular night, after reading a while, I curled up on my bed and with journal in hand, silently began to recite an angel prayer I had recited many times before.

>Angels of God, my Guardians dear
>For whom God's love commits me here,
>Ever this day be at my side
>To light and guard, to rule and guide
>Angels, please come to me

Lying in the darkness, I then asked the angels if they would please help me connect to Ray. I wrote that I loved him and missed him and how very painful it was to be "without" him. It was a release just to write to Ray, but within seconds, it was as if this conversation bubble appeared outside my head, maybe a foot up from my right eye, and Ray was talking to me. I didn't actually see his face with my physical eyes, but strongly sensed his face was there, as an extension of my third eye. It was Ray's voice and I could hear him clearly – including the intonations and pacing of his voice. (In the immediate future I would also be able to directly sense the feeling behind his words that expanded their meaning.) I started writing what he was saying to me, although I thought I definitely must be hearing things. It seemed crazy! How could this be happening? Was I just imagining, somehow, that I was hearing him in this way because, having been married to him for so long, I knew what he might say to me or to Liz and me in this situation? But the response was coming in such a relaxed way, quickly, without hesitation and so clearly – more rapidly and more clearly than my own thoughts would have come. I heard him say:

January 30, 2015

Do not worry, for I am with you always. I don't care to see you worrying and fretting, but would like to see you laughing and playing, for that is what I am doing here. Here there is life without pain, sorrow, grief, greed, annoyance, jealousy, financial worries or anything else negative that can be conjured.

I love you and know you love me. Open your hearts and minds to receive my love and love from all around you for there is so much coming your way.

I love you both and will be with you every step of the way, so do not fear. I am you and you are me. We are one and always will be.

Love, Ray

I froze for a moment and stared at the words on the page. While the voice, intonation and pacing were his, the word usage did *not* sound like Ray at all! Yet, it definitely did not sound like me either. There is no way I would have thought of a response like this. Playing along, I wrote, "Ray, this doesn't sound like you sounded on this Earth plane." He replied, "*Fewer interferences, clearer thoughts, clearer thinking – direct from God source.*"

Around this same time, there was another unusual occurrence. Our Christmas decorations included some infrared remote controlled candles. We used to place them in all the windows in the house. They could only be turned on by pointing the remote at one particular spot in the light bulb and honestly even then, nine out of ten times, they would not turn on. Immediately, in the couple weeks after Ray's passing, we had taken down all of the decorations except the window candles. They would have to be individually wrapped and I wasn't up to that. We didn't even attempt to turn them on, but left them in the windows.

One night, however, after eating, I noticed that the window candle in the spare room, where Liz and I slept, was on. Liz hadn't been home all day. The remote was on top of the piano in another room. I looked at the lit candle and thought, how odd! I hadn't turned it on! The candles couldn't go on by themselves. Was something wrong with it?

I picked up the remote and turned the candle off. (The candles always seemed to react to the off command well enough.) A few days passed and all of the window candles remained off except the light in the spare room, which was now on again, but why? I took out the batteries and put new ones in. I looked at the small amount of wiring. Nothing seemed to be compromised in any way. Why was this happening to this one candle? I tried and tried to think of a logical reason, but I was baffled. Then, all of a sudden, I started thinking about our Aunt Jean, Dad, Uncle Irv and Uncle Charles event and how I heard that people on the Other Side could make lights turn on and off. Could Ray possibly be turning that light on?

January 31, 2015

At approximately 10:00 pm, again, my daughter and I extinguished all the main bedroom lights and read in the dimly lit room. Again, before I slid under the covers, I took out my journal, said my angel prayer and again Ray "appeared" in that bubble diagonally above my right eye. Even though I could "see" him in this bubble and felt I could hear him speaking clearly and quickly to me as I scribbled his message, I had a great deal of difficulty believing that this communication was "real" and I was actually "hearing" him.

Journal entry:

P: Dearest Ray –
   Liz and I love you SO much!! We love you and just want to be with you.
R: *You will, in a shorter time than you think.*
P: And talk to you
R: *Just ask any questions and I can talk to you. I am not far away, but close at hand.*
P: Ray, did you turn on the artificial candle here in the bedroom?
R: *Of course I did.*
P: Sweetie – we miss you terribly. Nothing is good anymore – food isn't good, watching a film or being outside, riding in a car, going to bed, waking up – anything. Everything was made special because you were here and now you're not. What can you tell us?
R: *I love you both so much. You are in my thoughts all the time and I am watching over you. You make me happy when you laugh. I LOVE to hear you laugh, do you remember me saying that on Earth?*
P: Of course I do!
R: *Well, I still do and I want to hear it often, so don't disappoint me.*
P: But you made *us* laugh and we want to hear *you* laugh too! What or how do we get the opportunity to receive pleasure from being with *you* or sensing *you*?
R: *It will be in a different way, but we can still communicate. I will always be with you, remember that. I have not left, just transitioned and I will be part of your lives forever, my sweethearts. Rest. Allow yourselves to have peace. I love you.*
P: Can you make the window candle in here come on?
R: *I will try.* ☺ *I love you with all my heart.*
P: And we truly love you so. I love you, Ray!

Working through my angels each night before bed, I continued to write.

February 1, 2015

P: Dearest Ray,
   Liz and I love you and miss you so very much. On your side there is no pain, but on this side the hurt is deeply felt. Life is not nearly the same. I cry when I wake up and before I sleep. Life here, without you, is not beautiful or joyful anymore.
   What would you like us to know?

R: *I love you. I love you from the furthest depths of the ocean and beyond. You have told me I am your light and you two are mine. We will never be and are not separated. I can no longer be with you on your plane, but I **am** here! I am watching and helping and you will never be without me. Reach for me and our energy will intertwine.*

P: But I can't *feel* you, angel!

R: *I am here. The energy is more subtle, but I am here.*

P: We LOVE you! Do you see me crying?

R: *I do. I want you to smile for me.*

P: (I try to smile.) But I hurt, Ray. I love you and I miss you so…
   I can't touch you or feel you and I need you.

R: *Patricia (very lovingly), you and Liz **have** my love. You want my energy with you. It is yours. You want my touch. It will come to you in a variety of ways.….Please try not to think of what you're **missing** but what you **have**, like that glass half empty or full. You still have me. I may not be in the same exact form, but you still have me. I am alive and well and happy and with you. Try to behave as if you are with me.*
   There are jobs you must finish and you both will excel in what you do as I will help from this side.
   I am kissing you. I love you. I am with you. Grasp onto this and leave the negative thoughts behind.

WE ARE ONE!
WE ARE ONE!
WE ARE ONE!

As we are not separate, we are each other.
I love you both. Peace, my sweethearts. Kissing you and loving you.
Ray

During that first week in February, I continued to write to Ray each night. I was so exhausted emotionally and physically that when I finished writing, I never had any difficulty sleeping. Every morning I would wake up and within seconds feel the excruciating pain of the hole in my heart. I didn't necessarily want to get out of bed, but there were so many matters I needed to address – matters that either I, Ray, or Ray and I used to take care of together, that now belonged solely to me. I was *so* overwhelmed. I felt deluged. Everything was "the straw that broke the camel's back."

February 4, 2015

> P: Ray, guess who? I love you and Liz loves you so. (*crying*)
> Think you saw that I had a busy day today. I'm exhausted. I have been humming, "Never Can Say Good-bye girl" for a couple of weeks now and not understanding why. Then I was reading Patrick Mathews' book, *Never Say Good-bye*, and he was talking about spirits putting songs into your head to connect or having certain animals come to you.[1] (I love his book! It is *so* helpful.) There is a lone black crow whom I've named Gordon, who flies down to watch me walk out into the yard each day.
> Then, there are our candle lights going on in the spare room. I had asked you a few nights ago if you could turn the window

---

[1] Mathews, Patrick. *Never Say Goodbye*, Llewellyn Publications, 2010, pp.149-151.

candle on, and the next night on it went! I turned it off in the afternoon, and then it reignited again in the evening. OH MY GOSH, Ray! Is this you? I am **so** excited! I cannot tell you how happy I am that you are with me and us. I love you!

I am trying to smile and be happy. I understand that this raises our vibration and makes connections easier. I want to raise my vibration so we can be with each other more easily.

What would you like me to know?

R: *I love you and always will. I am with you all the time and tell Liz I love her so much and smile for me even if she doesn't want to. She has an awesome smile and I know she can do it. I wish she could have the best of both worlds like I do right now, but her turn will come and her child will be angry with her too.*

*You two are my treasures and I will **never** not hold you in my embrace. You are always in me. I am in and part of you. I love you!*

P: We love you angel and wish we could see you or feel your presence. I've read and heard in several places that people here can ask to feel the energy of a deceased loved one on their face or hand, for example. I would like to feel your energy on my right hand. Can we work on that together?

I love you.

R: *Sweet dreams, girls*

P: Our fullest love, angel. ☺

For years I had wanted to begin practicing meditation. All the spiritual classes Ray and I had taken, as well as the media, extolled its benefits. We had taken different types of meditation classes trying to find a technique that we could practice consistently, but had given up each time, feeling we just couldn't focus. A few times we had been presented with the idea of meditating and concentrating on what we could feel. So this night, I decided to do just that. Sitting on my bed, in our tiny spare room, I turned off all the lights but one, sat up straight, closed my eyes and asked Ray if he could let me feel his energy on my right hand. Taking three deep breaths to relax, I then focused on what I felt. As I zeroed in on each part of my body, I did at one point feel a very slight warm breeze wash over my hand. I knew it wasn't a draft. The heater was electric, so it wasn't coming from there either.

Could it be Ray? Oh my gosh, if it was, that would be so wonderful! Could our departed loved ones give us this type of sign? I decided to say thank you to him just in case, and went to bed.

The next night, when I wrote, I not only said thank you again for the possible energy sign, but for the spare room candle light that came on "by itself" (by Ray?) that same night.

His response February 5, 2015

Don't be shy about thinking that you are bothering me or I'm not listening. I can do everything here – multi-task to the nth degree without thinking – knowing about it – hearing all at once. So talk away. I love being included in what you and Liz do!

And we *loved* "being" with him!

February 6, 2015

P: Dear angels,
    May I please speak to Ray?

P: Ray?? I love you! Liz loves you too!
R: *I love both of you so much.*
P: I miss you so…
R: *I miss you too, babe, but I **am** with you and Liz.*
P: What would you like me to know today?

R: Girls – I love you so. I love you bigger and more than your mind can ever imagine—that's what love feels like here—it has no boundaries—no beginning and no end and completely engulfs you.

P: Then we are sending that right back to you to envelop you with an extra dose.
It's painful here a lot of the time. We miss you!

R: It is so much more beautiful here than you can ever imagine—but I want you to try. With fields of emeralds and golds and words that are not spoken but completely understood and butterflies the likes you have never seen. Animals that you can communicate with telepathically. Imagine the most beautiful things you can and they are here... Who are you sad for?

P: For us

R: Why?

P: You are our favorite light and it's hard to see you.

R: But remember I **am** here. You can...or if not yet...learn to feel my energy. You have my love, my light, my energy – my essence with you.

P: I know you are right.
I will try...
Goodnight angel

R: Goodnight beautiful girls

February 7, 2015

P: Dear Ray –
You must be having such a wonderful time on the Other Side. Sounds like everything you could ever wish for is available to you. You deserve it. You worked very hard here. I am happy for you, although words cannot describe how much Liz and I miss you. Your entire light is missed and nothing holds the same value anymore because we don't have you physically here to share things with. What would you like Liz and me to know?

R: Patty, Pat, Pat, Pat, Patricia
(Whispering) I………………….Loveeeeee…………………
…..Youuuuu………….

P: I wish there was some way for you to know and comprehend how very much I love you. Maybe you can over there. I just can't on this side. But with every cell in my body, I love you, always have and always will.

R: *Patricia—I love you with all my heart. Being on another plane doesn't stop that. It could never stop that. Love transcends all boundaries. Love is energy. My love encompasses you and will never leave. You are engulfed by it and drawn into it…*
Don't forget it and don't doubt for one second. I love you and you are my life. You are a part of me and always will be. Where I go, so do you. Stop thinking of us as separate. None of God's creations are separate – just all part of the same fabric.
*Do not speak as if I am somewhere never to return, when I am here constantly. You will never get rid of me. You will never lose me. You will never be without me. I will never **not** be part of you. We are intertwined and will be so throughout eternity.*

P: (With tears) I love you sweetie and Liz does too!
I hoped we would have more time to relax and play during retirement. I guess we will, but in a different way, and I have to learn to enjoy you in this way.

R: *Give Liz a kiss for me and a hug*

Each day, in addition to writing in my journal, I would turn off the spare room candle light, and in the wee hours of the morning, I would wake up to find that it was on again. Sometimes the light was off and I would be in the throes of tears – crying, when all of a sudden, the light would go on and flicker, as if to comfort me –as if Ray was saying, "I am here." Other times, it would turn on just before Liz and I climbed into our beds – just before we turned the other lights off. Still other times, I would need to make a decision about something regarding the house, for example. Outdoors, there were things that needed to be revamped so that I could take care of them on my own. They were decisions Ray and I would have made together since this was his area of expertise. Sometimes the smallest decisions would seem so overwhelming because I was already emotionally and physically shredded. As I lay in bed, batting my options back and forth, crying, and then reaching a possible conclusion, all of a sudden the light would "magically" start to pulse quickly on and off as if to say, "YES, YES, that is the best route—YOU'VE GOT IT!!" It might then immediately go off or stay on for a few hours and extinguish itself.

Whether it was hearing Ray or "connecting" via candle light, all of this seemed so completely unbelievable at the time, and even as I'm writing this it seems as if my previous understanding of "reality" would agree. But yes, IT WAS TRUE! And I would cry! I couldn't fathom how this could *possibly* be happening, but in part because of the timing, I truly believed it was Ray! It *had* to be Ray! How else and why else could this be happening with such regularity **now**? Nothing like this had EVER happened before! It all started right after Ray passed (and we had the lights a year before this.)

I did begin to realize how much weight we place on what we see, feel and sense—but primarily *see* in this world, as if it was the only sense we have. And **why** do we place the most emphasis on this sense?

Chapter Seven
Enhanced Communication

I needed and wanted to be with Ray. He had passed, yet he was still "alive?" In order for me to reconcile Ray's still being "alive" without his physical presence, I needed to experience him through as many senses as possible. He was communicating his presence and his love for us through my journaling, the candlelight, songs in my head, and dreams. He was demonstrating to us over and over again, just in the few weeks since his passing that he was still "alive," cared about us and could still be with us. Given the circumstances, what more could I want? Yet, being human, I guess I wanted more. It was so difficult to wrap my head around everything that had happened and was happening with Ray right now. I wanted to experience him almost as fully as when he was here alongside us, to be able to truly believe and appreciate this gift, even though it seemed unrealistic. But what was unrealistic anymore?

February 11, 2015

> P: Dear angels,
> May I please speak to Ray?
> R: *(Whispering) I………………………*
>   *Loveeeeeee……………………..*
>   *Youuuuuuuu……………………*
> P: (Crying) I love you so much! It's so hard for me to think of you as being on the Other Side. I'm not happy about that. I *am* happy for you in that you are in the most beautiful place ever and you

deserve the very best, but I'm sad for me and for Liz.

It's very empty here. I know I can speak to you and this *does* help and I can't thank you enough for making the candlelight come on in the spare room – today it came on at 6:00 pm. Thank you **so** much!

I feel so empty. I know Liz does too. I want so badly to feel your presence – your energy.

R: *Reiki will do it and meditation. Try one of Patrick Mathews' meditations, too, if you like.*

P: I will. I think about going on vacation with you – to our spot. I know. I know. You tell me you'll be there, but I can't *see* you and right now I can't feel you or maybe I doubt when I do.

R: *This is new. I can help. You need to learn. It will help you and others.*

P: Well then, I need to learn **fast** sweetie, really **fast**.

R: *I love you. Please don't cry. It puts up a border that can be difficult to cross. Try to be happy or content or peaceful. It must be hard for you. You tell me it is, but Patricia, Elizabeth, girls, I am really with you and I can be with you every step of the way. You have to trust me and trust the Universe.*

P: (I continue to cry, completely wrapped up in myself and grief)

R: **PAT!!!** *(He shouted and shook me with his words. My tears froze.)* **WE'VE LEARNED SO MUCH TOGETHER! WHY NOT THIS? WHY WON'T YOU DO THIS WITH ME?**

(In this moment he stunned me into absolute belief that **THIS WAS HIM!** I had been the initiator in our taking so many spiritual classes. Now, he was asking me to connect in this way – trusting it was him and trusting in him as we embarked on this new adventure together. Yet I was hesitating because of doubt? In this moment the idea seemed preposterous!)

R: *Why not let me teach you and Liz and open yourself up?*

P: I am open in my mind. You were always better on this plane at letting go and opening to Spirit. I want to. I truly do, but I need

help. Please help me over the hurdle to give me direction.
You mentioned meditation? How??

R: *Pretend you are holding my hands and trust me completely and let me take you where you need to go with this.*

> *So imagine yourself sitting and placing both your hands in mine. Relax. Let go. Breathe and focus on your breath.*
> *Try this for ten minutes each day.*

P: I will. I love you Raymond and I know Liz does too. She loves you so much and we just sit in sadness and disbelief of what has happened.

R: *Give each other lots of hugs. Please give yourself physical hugs from me and love each other. And remember, you may not be able to see me, but I am here and always with you, alongside so many people on this side who love you and can't wait for you to open up to receive all this love we have to give you! Hurry up! We're getting impatient! We're excited!*

P: I love you, Raymond, and Liz loves you too!!

I tried to meditate as Ray had suggested and for the first time in my meditation "career," I was truly able to do this without constantly losing focus. I LOVED it! The ten minutes would go by *so* quickly.

During this time, I also felt closer to Ray and it gave me a great deal of peace and comfort. We decided to make a date to do this each night before journaling.

February 13, 2015

P: Dear angels,
May I please speak to Ray?

Enhanced Communication

P: Ray!! Liz said that because you always gave me flowers for Valentine's Day, she asked you if you wanted her to get flowers for me today. You responded YES immediately with a red-tailed hawk – your favorite bird—flying overhead.
Thank you, sweetie! You must have seen me cry when I received the flowers. I LOVE YOU SO MUCH!
I wanted to write a Valentine's Day card from both of us to Liz. What would you like to say to her?

R: *I love you, Liz, very much. I know it's so hard for you right now to understand what has transpired and how it could ever possibly get better. But as you develop our new relationship, it won't be the same as before, that's for sure, but you will be able to feel the intensity of my love for you—stronger and stronger—and I know it will make you happy. Please continue to open yourself up to me and all the love I have for you because I don't want it to stop just because you can't see me. That love energy is there and directed to you all the time and always will be. I want your Mom to give you a ton of kisses from me today. I love you both very much and I know you love me…*
and Pat – you've been thinking about reinventing the summer vacation we planned by going on a short healing cruise to the Bahamas with Barb and Jan. I LOVE IT! I LOVE IT! Thank you for thinking of them. It will be nice. You'd do OK. I will be there too. I know Liz says she doesn't want to go right now but I'll help her to want to go. So tell her not to hog my side of the bed! ☺

P: But would your sisters go?

R: *They will go.*

P: I love you, Ray.

R: *I love you.*

Chapter Eight
Turning Point

On February 11th, Ray had stunned me into the belief that I was indeed connecting with him, when, during our evening exchange he forcefully called me to task. Being the doubter that I was, however, I was still having difficulty wrapping my complete faith and belief around the fact that I was actually communicating with him on the Other Side. Until… February 16, 2015.

It was around 11:00 pm – time for bed. After turning most of the lights off, once again I curled up on my bed to meditate/sit in stillness with Ray and then journal in the dimly lit room. Per routine, after meditation, I recited my angel prayer, took some deep breaths and asked to be connected to Ray. He "appeared" and I began to write.

P: Ray – I'm here again. I love you so much, sweetie.
R: *I love you my sweetheart. Look at me!!... I love you!*
P: What would you like to share with me today?
R: *The sun, moon and stars are just a small part of the Universe. It's people like you who make up the rest of the glowing part of the Universe. Your happiness makes me happy. Remember how I love to see you smile.*
P: I wish I could think up the beautiful things you say. You mean so much to me and I would love to shower you with words or feelings that show you how much I love you.
R: *I **do** feel them and I felt that one. It was great!*

P: I'm so glad. I love you!
R: *Well, I love you and I'm telling you we won't be apart that long. So get working on your projects.*
Drumming? You could come to me via a journey.
You know how I love the Grand Canyon and Sedona. You could take Bill and Dan there. They need to see this and Laurelle's Crystal Shop and (chuckling) *the Blue Bird… "Inn"* ☺ (another chuckle like "Inn" is not at all the word he wants, but he is just going to plug in anything so he can continue… it's Blue Bird "something".)
P: Blue Bird "Inn"? (*Drifting away for a few seconds, I thought… 'we have **never** been to a Blue Bird Inn or Blue Bird anything in Arizona. What could he be talking about?'*)
R: *Yeah* (chuckles), *something like that …about 30 minutes outside Phoenix….and…El Tovar. You know the spots. They would love them and I would love watching you show them and being with all of you.*
P: Okay… *(hesitating – hearing Ray say this was SO real!)* We'll see. ☺ Anything else?
R: *Tell Liz I love her and to try to be happy. I need to ride on her happiness. I can feel it here.*
P: I'll tell her. I love you, baby -- SO MUCH!

My pen was in mid-air. I was confounded. One of Ray's favorite spots in the whole world was the Grand Canyon. We had been maybe 5-6 times. He only ever had two weeks' vacation every year and didn't want to use all his vacation time on "one vacation." If we traveled to Arizona, we wanted to visit relatives as well. As such, we basically followed the same itinerary each time. We flew to Phoenix, rented a car and drove immediately to Sedona, nonstop. In Sedona, we stayed over a night, then drove to the south rim of the Grand Canyon and stayed a night or two before heading south, to Tucson. We **never ever** visited or stayed at any Blue Bird Inn or Blue Bird anything!

The rest of his dialogue made sense, though – very much so and it sounded as always, **exactly** like him, as if he was right next to me – just over my right eye!

It was around midnight. I was alone in the dark room. Instead of my usual sliding under the covers after writing, I meandered over to the computer and slowly sat down. Could there possibly be a Blue Bird "something" thirty minutes outside Phoenix? I remembered Sylvia Browne saying that our loved ones on the Other Side are capable of travel. Several years in the future, I would see a film that discussed precisely that. Had Ray visited the Grand Canyon since transitioning and did he find a place called the Blue Bird ___ that he wanted Bill and Dan to see?

I turned on the computer and decided to google "Blue Bird Inn, 30 minutes outside of Phoenix." There was more hesitation than usual on the screen, and then the **only** item that came up was the Blue Bird Rock and Curio Shop approximately 30 minutes outside of Phoenix. We had NEVER been to a Blue Bird Rock and Curio shop in Arizona!

I clicked on the link and up came a picture of a small, almost makeshift looking, very typical "country" side-of-the-road rock shop, like I had often seen on my travels with Ray. My eyes locked on the words, "NATIVE AMERICAN JEWELRY" in big letters across the front of the shop. I then laughed for several reasons. One, Ray loved rocks. One of our first dates, years ago, had been to a lapidary show. Ray had also worked in stone design for years and thoroughly enjoyed it. If we had time on vacation, (which often we did not), he truly enjoyed being able to wander into a shop like this, chatting with the store owner and purchasing a stone or two. He *always* had stones in his pants' pockets –stones he thought were interesting in some way and I usually ended up picking them out of our washing machine. Another reason for the giggle, was that Bill and Dan were both fascinated with rocks and crystals and there is no doubt in my mind that Ray would have enjoyed stopping at a shop like this with them. And finally, I chuckled because Ray and I had this ongoing discussion about Native American jewelry. He really loved it and wanted to buy me some. I liked the designs and the stones, but felt that the settings were generally too big and overpowering for someone my size. He never gave up hope, though. Every time we were in a shop that sold Native American jewelry, he would search and ask me if *this* was the "right" piece or *that one*. So, here he was again, I thought, enjoying his stones and looking for a piece of jewelry for me. I smiled and my eyes filled with tears.

I don't know exactly how long I was sitting in that dark room, alone, in front of the computer screen staring motionless at the photo of that shop. All of this seemed completely (and here are those words again, dear reader) "unbelievable" – "crazy," but this was real! I was hearing Ray! He was talking to me! I was now **so excited** – walking on air, I could hardly sleep. How *could* this be real?

February 17, 2015

P: Dear angels,
May I please speak to Ray?

Ray?? Ray??
R: *I'm here. Don't fret. I'm here.*
P: You didn't turn the candle light on today.
R: *Hey, I have to keep you guessing. I don't want you to know everything I know…* ☺
P: I remember when you used to say something like that followed by, "then you'd be as smart as me." ☺ I think your dad said that.
R: *Pat, Patricia – my beautiful baby. I'm right here next to you.*
P: I sure hope so. What would you like to share with me today?
R: *Let's see. I'm not sure how to say this, but sometimes I feel as though you're not listening to me.* ☺
P: Are you giving me a dose of my own medicine? (*When Ray was on this plane, I would often chide him for this.*)

R: Yes…☺

P: Well, I guess I deserve it. Not listening to you as you are now?

R: Yes

P: Well, you have to train me. I'm not used to this physical/spirit relationship. I need help. I want to learn and would love to help other people feel connected to their loved ones, but I need your help. Do we have a deal?

R: *We do! Done!*

P: OK, partner, let's do it! I'm ready and willing! Love you, angel!

R: *Love you and tell Liz I love her.*

P: I will.

February 19, 2015

The candle in the spare room had been off all day. Around 6:00 pm tonight, the candle light went on. I talked to Ray again about wanting to be able to feel his energy and heighten my awareness. He said that I needed to eat more fruits and vegetables and try to stay away from too much sugar, although he knew I had a "sweet tooth." I told him how it was so hard, now, because I didn't get pleasure in anything without him and I kept trying to find something to make me happy – that nothing made me as happy as his "sweetie pie" self. ☺ His response was, "Well, I'm always that way now, so you should be at your happiest!" (*Darn that guy! He got me!*)

The candle light stayed on all night. I turned it off in the morning.

Next night, February 20th, after Ray and I finished talking – around 10:00 pm, I began to cry. When my father had passed years ago, I remembered crying steadily for about three months and then it subsided and stopped. This time, though, I had no 24/7 support system. There was no one to support me consistently because that had been Ray. Liz was sometimes at home and often not. She had to deal with her father's grief in her own way. When the tears came, it felt like they were emanating from the deepest part of my soul.

I went to bed. Tired from crying, I fell asleep but woke around 2:00 am. Feeling very depressed and restless, I got out of bed and decided to make a cup of tea. I asked Ray, out loud, to be with me. When I went back upstairs, the candle light in the spare room (which had been off all day) was now on. I sat with Ray's candle – with him, until I fell asleep. In the morning, I turned the light off, did some housework, and when I returned to the spare room, the light was on again.

February 23, 2015

    P: Dear angels,
         May I please speak to my husband, Ray?

         Ray, do you know how much I love you? As deep as the ocean and more.
    R: *I know. I love you sooooo much.*
    P: I know. What do you want me to know or what would you like to teach me today?
    R: *The Universe is so wide and so huge and complex, it is difficult to comprehend, but the best way to describe it is to say that it is beyond human understanding. There are so many facets, but to you I will say that there are energetic strands that connect all parts of the Universe to the core – the essence. It is not necessary to understand fully, just realize that we are indeed all part of one being – all part of the universal web of life and each part needs to do its part for the complete survival of the whole.*
        Every single particle of the thread is just as important as the next – no particle more or less important than the one that resides next to it.

Love One Another
Help One Another
Respect and Honor One Another
For the Betterment of the Whole

Pat – I love you. I love Liz. Please give my love to your mom. All of you are so dear to me. I am with you, watching over you and caring for you.
With deepest love,
Ray

As the days passed, Liz and I continued to tell Ray how much we loved and missed him, and he continued to reiterate how much he loved and treasured us. He constantly reminded us that we were never without him. He was with us every moment.

When Ray was on the Earth plane, the three of us used to love to travel. He now relayed that, having been given the travel bug, he was continuing to do this on the Other Side, making new friends and renewing old ties. He also told us he had people to introduce us to and that he was so excited at the thought of being able to show us around and take us to all kinds of places. He informed us that he was happier than he had ever been, busy doing so many things. There was, he said, so much to do and so much to learn, it was fascinating.

He continued to turn the candlelight in our spare room on by request or at his whim. Once, while writing and reiterating how happy and grateful I was to have that light because it was the *only* tangible thing I *had* of his, he interjected with a smile, "What about my pants?" (*Always the jokester, I still had his jeans and khakis hanging in our closet.*) He then continued by saying that if I needed still other tangible signs from him, "Then take pictures!"

In an effort to "do" something, other than cry, worry, and feel overwhelmed with legalities, house care concerns, work, etc., I looked for other books to read on grief. I read a second book by Patrick Mathews. I thoroughly enjoyed it and decided, now, that I would very much like to have a reading with him. I had never had a reading with a medium before, but if I was going to do this for the first time, I wanted him/her to be highly regarded in their profession.

My daughter had a reading with Patrick several years prior and thought very highly of him. So, I decided to try to make an appointment.

His book provided a website. On visiting the website, I discovered that Patrick Mathews was so sought after – his readings were in such high demand, that they were now by lottery only. My heart fell. I was so disappointed, but when I told my daughter what happened, she urged me to just "give it a try." I had nothing to lose. She was right, in a way, but why would *I* have a chance at winning the lottery?

On the website, we were asked for an email address and name. We were told that within a week or so we would be informed of the results. I looked up to Ray and said, "Honey, I'm trying to get us an appointment with Patrick Mathews, but it's by lottery. If you want us to have this opportunity to connect, you are going to have to push to the front of the line and make it happen."

Well, much to my complete surprise, on the third day after I filled out the form, I opened my mailbox to find an email from the Patrick Mathews' group. My daughter and I had an appointment near the end of April! It was now February. To say I was elated would have been an understatement.

Chapter Nine

Coming to Terms

I was about to begin work again. I was a little nervous. A twelve hour a day work schedule was coupled with everything else life, and now death, placed on the table. Could I handle it? I had to.

When I wrote to Ray the evening before I returned to work, I expressed my concern and he wrote:

I'll be with you both every step of the way, holding your hands and bringing you comfort. Yes, I will try for joy too. I love you both so much, my girls, and I will never leave you alone. You will never be alone although you may think you are because you do not see me with your eyes. I will take care of you. (Promise)

We really are still a strong threesome, but in a different way. We still are working together. We still are inseparable. We still are part of each other and no one can break us apart. **No one** *and* **nothing** *can break our bond. It is way too strong!*

I love you.
I know you love me.
Love is the strongest bond there is.

I thanked him for his love and support. I also thanked him for the lit candle in our room, which meant so much that night. I then began my new nightly ritual of signing off my correspondence by drawing a heart with two or three small hearts inside.

March 2, 2015

Work went well for both Liz and I. We were blessed with the most wonderful, caring people to work beside, and they made everything so much easier. The hollow feeling – for Liz, "a void" – was ever present. I felt like a shell and didn't know how to begin to fill it without Ray. Thank goodness for meditation. When I meditated, I would do as he suggested – imagine that I was placing my hands in his and then surrender and focus on my breathing. Sometimes, instead of focusing on my breathing, I would picture *him* in my mind's eye and focus on *him*. I could feel extra energy surrounding my hands. It was heavenly. I truly felt he was with me.

March 3, 2015

>Dear angels,
>   May I please speak to Ray?
>P: Ray…is that you?
>R: *I'm right next to you.*
>P: If I place my right hand out, could you touch it?
>R: *Better than that, I can hold it if you like.*
>P: I would **love** that!
>R: *(smiles)…I haven't left you, remember.*
>P: Yes, I have to think that way. Anything you'd like to share with me?
>R: *Pat, you are a smart, competent person. I have every faith that you can do whatever it takes to survive until we are together – to thrive— to do what you need.*
>P: But I wanted to do *this* with you.
>R: *You* ***are*** *doing this with me, but it is better this way. You may not be able to understand, but trust me.*

P: … I love you so much it hurts.
R: *Well, if you do, you must want to make me happy, and if **that** is true, then you need to smile and be happy for your happiness is my happiness.*
P: I'll try, but nothing is the same without you.
R: *Soon you will be able to sense my love in other ways. Keep working on connecting. You can do this!*
P: Please help me…

No candlelight today. Maybe when I go to bed, can you turn it on?
R: *I'll try. I love you.*
P: I love you.

The candlelight became extremely important to me. I felt it was the only concrete evidence I had of Ray's existence. But was I just being gullible or naïve? Was there actually a pattern to the light going on and off or something else causing the light's behavior pointing to some sort of mechanical failure? Yet, the candlelight didn't go on every day. Sometimes it didn't go on for days. And the light didn't go on and/or off at the same times either. It often lit when I asked or when I needed reassurance most. It was as if the light had a mind of its own.

After writing on March 3rd and asking for the light, I pulled down the window shade over the unlit candle before I went to bed. When I woke at 10:30 pm, having difficulty sleeping that evening, the candle was on. I was thrilled! When the alarm sounded in the morning, however, it was off.

March 4, 2015

After we exchanged our I love yous and my gratitude for his always being with me, I asked Ray during journaling, if he had any information he wanted to share with me today. He began:

R: *I love the way you smile. I love the way you laugh. I love your curly hair.*

P: I love the way you say that and I wish I could hear you in person.

R: *You hear me this way – with your inner ear. Remember how I had to hear a slightly different way with hearing aids? Well, you are hearing a different way and don't complain.* ☺
Remember how you told me I needed to adjust? Now you do ☺ *and you can do this.*

P: O.K.…will you help me?

R: *You bet your knickers!* ☺

P: (Startled by this rejoinder, I smiled. I hadn't heard him use that phrase in years!)

I meditated tonight. At the end of the meditation Ray told me that 'instead of journeying out' (I love to travel); 'it was now time to journey within.'

Also – when I came home from school around 4/4:30 today and went upstairs, the candlelight in the spare room, which had been off when I left for work, was now lit.

March 5, 2015

As always, I asked the angels for help with "my connection." I expressed my gratitude for the candlelight and then I wrote:

P: Dearest Ray –
I felt lots of energy by my face and hands during meditation tonight. I think that must be you.
R: I'm proud of you. You're working **with** me. Don't be afraid. Just let go.
P: Please help me.
R: You can **do** this! We've let go with Reiki and healing classes with Alberto. It's easy. Three deep breaths and put yourself in my hands, the angels and God's. Nothing can harm you. You are ready to go.
P: O.K.…I'll do my best.
Anything in particular you would like me to know?
R: (whispering) I……………………
Loveeeeee…………………..
Youuuuuuu ……………………….
P: I love **you**. You speak to me with such logic about accepting what I have to with you and I am trying my best to follow your lead.
R: Good! Look at my face and trust. Take my hand and trust. You will be fine and I am here completely – maybe **more** completely than before. I can do whatever you need.
P: I need YOU!
R: You **have** me!

March 6, 2015

Driving home tonight after school, and feeling down, I asked Ray if he could turn the candlelight on in the spare room. When Liz and I drove into the driveway, the light in the spare room, which was off in the morning, was now on.

March 7, 2015

    P: Dear Ray –
Anything in particular you'd like to share with me? Please know that I *love* having you with me.

    R: *OK, I'll tell you a story.*

    P: (I always loved stories and when I was little I used to begin a story with "once aponce a time.")

    R: *Once aponce a time, there was a beautiful girl whom I married. She had curly hair and the cutest smile. I loved her and still do.*

    P: I love you.

    R: *Well, her hubby had to leave on a little vacation. He wouldn't be gone long before they'd be together again, but it seemed long. So her hubby said, "Don't worry. Be the strong person you are and hold down the fort. Just take care of things as you normally do and we'll be together soon." It was simple. That's what she did and all was well. It was simple.*

Pat, make it simple, not complicated. Just do what you need to do to get the job done and relax a little. Don't work hard. I'm relaxing and it's good. We'll all be together soon. You and Liz have projects to finish – work to accomplish to help others and I will be helping from here. We are a dynamite threesome and always will be.

*I'm here. I'm with you. You are with me. All for one and one for all. We can **do** this! I'm by your side every second. Trust me. Believe in me. I love you both SO much! I'll be there every second. Just reach and I am here. Remember that!*

    P: I love you! ☺

During meditation tonight, I started thinking about dancing with Ray. We used to dance quite often at home. He would hum a ballad, while we held each other and moved to the music. As I sat in the dimly lit room, I felt *so* strongly that he was with me. I stood up and carrying that song in my head, started to move to the music, "pretending" he was there too. I could feel cool energy down my entire left side as if he was standing next to me and we were dancing together. I was *so* happy!

March 9, 2015

A month ago, Ray informed me that his sisters would agree to go on our proposed healing cruise to the Bahamas. They had not only lost their brother this year, but their mother, as well. I just heard from them today. He was right! They are interested!

He was also correct when he told me that Liz, who had definitely been hesitant about coming along, would change her mind and decide to join us. She has!

I also had my misgivings about this trip. I wasn't certain that, emotionally, I could handle Ray's absence on a summer vacation that was supposed to include him, as well. I wanted him to be there too. His response:

R: *Pat, I'll be there…You will be wrapped in my energy and so will Liz.*
P: Would it be in my best interest to go?
R: *I think so. I'll take care of my two girls. You don't have to worry.*
P: We had wanted to have fun with you too.
R: *Heavenly pleasures far outweigh earthly pleasures and I can give you heavenly pleasures. Connect with me and see. Feel, believe, let yourself and your senses be enveloped. Haven't you enjoyed our dancing? My hands in yours during meditation? Is that better, worse or the same as a Disney ride?*
P: Better…O.K.…so
R: *Think about that*
P: I love you, honey.
R: *I love you too and I'll never leave you.*
P: I'm counting on that.

March 11, 2015

Dear angels,
    May I please speak to Ray?

P: Dearest Ray,
    I still cannot believe that you are on the Other Side.
R: *I know how sad you feel and I don't like to see you this way, but truly the bigger picture is so beautiful. Wait, you will see and I am here for you and will be with you every second there and every second here… There will be so many surprises, beauty and joy.*
P: Our biggest joy will be you, you know.
R: *Well…I think I can say the same, but there are so many people and pets who are anxious to have you beside them. Don't worry. No rush, but we're here and are with you there **too**. Know that we all love you, tend to your needs and enjoy seeing you and all the beautiful things Liz and you do. You're on the right track. Keep going. We encompass you with love every day and every minute.*
P: I love you so….I do miss your being physically here with us.
R: *Concentrate on the now and our connection. The grief counselor will have a new source to make it stronger.*
P: I am open. I love you.
R: *Love you too – so much. Feel me close. I am here.*

March 12, 2015

Well, just as Ray had informed me, the grief counselor (much to my surprise), introduced me to a new way of connecting with him today. It was a method I had never heard of before, called "kything," outlined in a book entitled, *Kything: The Art of Spiritual Presence*, by Louis M. Savary and Patricia

H. Berne.[2] It was actually a variation on a connection method I was already using. She lent me the book and I decided to give some of the ideas a try. In some ways, it definitely helped me feel more present with Ray.

At night I wrote:

    P: Dear angels,
           May I please speak to Ray?

    P: Ray…as always, sweetie, I am sending and giving you my love. I'm tired today. Do you get tired on the Other Side?
    R: *I wish you would never get tired as I am not, here. When you retire, I hope things are easy. Tried to set them up so they would be. Try not to worry about everything and anything. I will help, my precious girl. You work too hard and worry too much. Try to take it easy and enjoy the moment. Look inward and discover your divineness. Look up and discover the stars; down – the earth and across – the trees and plants. This is your new adventure and I will take you there.*
    P: Please hold my hand and be with me on this journey.
    R: *You betcha I will. Wouldn't miss that for the world.*

March 13, 2015

Note: When I came home from school today, the light was on.

That night, working through the angels as always, I wrote:

    P: Ray??? I love you.
    R: *I love you too. Where are you feeling pain? I can help.*
    P: Right now, in my head. I think I just want to be surrounded by your energy and feel loved and protected.

---

2   Savary. Louis M., and Patricia H. Berne. *Kything: The Art of Spiritual Presence*, Paulist Press, 1988, p. 3.

R: *I'm always here surrounding you and protecting you, loving you and trying to keep you safe from harm.*
P: I love you so…thank you so much for everything. What would you like to tell me about today?
R: *The moon is so bright.*
P: (The shades were three fourths down and I hadn't seen it.)
R: *It looks so beautiful. Look at it with me.*
P: (It was so cloudy; at first I couldn't see it). I can't find the moon. Oh…it is a full moon. It's pretty cloudy, but it *is* bright out there - outside it *is* bright.
I will stand next to your candle in the window and look outside with you.
R: *I will wrap my arms and my energy around you.*
P: It's a deal! What would you like me to know?
R: *I am brighter than the brightest star and I shine. You can access me in your head, your heart and your soul. I am here. You know that when you meditate you can feel me.*
P: I *think* I do sometimes.
I love you. Thank you for the candlelight and for being here.
I sleep better knowing you're with me.

March 15, 2015

P: Ray… I love you…
R: *I wish I could help you to understand how much I need to see you happy. It helps me to be closer. I know it's difficult. I know you need to work through things, but happiness and raising your vibration can bring us closer.*
Patricia – Try. Try sweetie…You can do this!
P: I will start doing Reiki again to mend my heart. Maybe then I can make better progress.

March 16, 2015

Both Ray and I were very fond of Reiki. It had become an integral part of our lives for fifteen years. I had been teaching Reiki classes for a while. Now, even though I had more than enough to occupy my time, I was debating about whether or not to continue teaching. I *loved* the idea of sharing Reiki with others. It had so much to offer and had certainly proved to be very beneficial in helping me to sense Ray's energy. I felt excited about the prospect of giving a class, although depressed about Ray's absence. We had learned Reiki together, become Masters together and talked about teaching together.

It was late afternoon as I sat in the spare room mulling over what path I should pursue. All of a sudden, the candlelight, which had been off, turned on and started pulsing wildly as if, in response to my thoughts, it was saying, **"Yes, teach Reiki!"** If Ray's spirit – Ray's energy – wasn't behind this candle's conduct, why or how could this be happening right now – at this moment? I started to laugh.

I left the room to wash my hair. When I returned, the candlelight wasn't pulsing, but remained steady. It then went out. Later in the evening, when I returned to the room once again after getting ready for bed, the light was on once more.

I wrote to Ray:

P: Dear angels,
May I please speak to Ray?
R: *I'm right here. You didn't need to call. I'm focused and paying attention – not like on the Earth plane. I am all yours, my beautiful baby. Did you notice my lights?*
P: I did and I am so grateful!
I love you, cutie!

R: *(whispering) I............................*
    Loveeee............................
    Youuuuuuu...........................
    Do I get a smile?
P: (I smiled – a big smile)
R: *That's my girl. I expect to see lots of those from now on. We are partners and always will be. We're just doing our work differently right now. Did you notice I was applauding your decision to do Reiki?*
P: I thought that might be it, but wasn't sure.
R: *Be sure. I'll help.*
P: I know you will.
R: *Help is my middle name.*
P: I love you forever, Raymond. ☺

March 17, 2015

The candlelight stayed on all night. I turned it off before going to work. After work, Liz and I met some friends for dinner at an Italian restaurant at 4:00. When we drove in the driveway at 6:00 and I looked up at the spare room window, the candlelight was on. What a wonderful welcome sight! It was as if Ray was welcoming us home!

At night I wrote:

P: Ray??? I can't see you with my eyes, but the candlelight is on, which means to me that you are here. I love you so.
R: *I............................*
    Loveeeeee....................
    Youuuuuuuuu............................
P: Feels like you are saying this in my ear
R: *I am.* ☺

P: Thank you so much for being here. I don't know how I'd survive if you didn't do this. What would you like to share with me today?

R: *Pat, I am here for you and please take advantage of connecting with me. I want to connect with you. I love you – cherish you and want to give you as much love as possible and I have even more love to give you now than before. The soul can carry so much more love than your physical body. That is what I carry and send to you. There is unlimited love here that envelops, protects, emanates from everything – pure unadulterated love and it is yours to connect with. Open your souls and receive my love and the love the Universe and hereafter have to offer. I shall try my best and I want you to do the same. You will be surprised and so overwhelmed.*

P: I am trying, but I'm not sure how.

R: *Keep meditating and **do not give up**. It will come and the higher your vibration, the easier for me to ride on that vibration to connect. I am yours. You are mine. Our souls are intertwined and will always continue to be. Love, remember, is the strongest bond there is. **Nothing** can break it. No matter what. You **love** me. I **love** you. I **love** Liz. She **loves** me. This is our steel bridge. No one can tear it down. I love you and always will.*

P: I love you and always will.

As always, I signed off by drawing a heart with two or three small hearts inside (labeled with our names).

March 26, 2015

P: Ray?

R: *I am here.*

P: I love you so.

I miss you.
I hope I'm really communicating with you.
R: *Why do you doubt?*
P: If I *am* communicating with you, could I please see a pig?
R: *Not me…* ☺
P: (Rolling my eyes and shaking my head). Sweetie, no! Don't even joke about that!
R: *OK, Just trying to bring a little levity to the situation.* ☺
P: I apologize. I know. You're cute. I'm just trying to figure this out and I miss you.
R: *Patricia, Patricia, Patricia…*
You need to come to terms.
I've told you so many times.
Love never dies.
P: Ray, I think part of the heaviness I feel, too, is because I'm overwhelmed – school, thinking about financial stability, the care of the house. This is a lot for me. I don't know how to do all the things you did to take care of the house – electrical, plumbing, construction. It's very stressful.
You're doing a GREAT job of supplying us with people coming to our rescue. Thanks so much! No one could have done better.
R: *At your service.*
P: Sweetie – anything else you want to share?
R: *I love you.*
P: I love you.

March 28, 2015

I gave my first Reiki class since Ray's passing. Coincidentally? one of the students had a family member who was going through a medical situation very similar to the one Ray was in right before he passed. Her family member was now in the same hospital, in the same unit that Ray had been and having a great deal of difficulty.

Last night I asked Ray if he could join me for this class. The candlelight, which had been off, immediately came on – blinking as if to say YES! While giving the class, I felt I could hear Ray reminding me to tell certain Reiki stories – stories he undoubtedly would have told had he been there. I felt like he was co-teaching the class with me.

The candlelight stayed on all last night, throughout the day during the class, and went off somewhere around 8/9:00 pm this evening.

On the 26th, I had asked Ray to validate I was hearing him, by showing me "a pig." On television today, I saw a whole *group* of pigs! I laughed. I guess I *am* hearing you, Ray!

March 29, 2015

    Dear angels,
        May I please speak to Ray?

P: Ray!! I love you. I'm wondering if I connected with your spirit tonight. If not, I will keep practicing. It feels like I'm connecting.
R: *You **are** connecting. I can feel it. I look forward to it every day. Want "a kiss"?*
P: Bet I do.
R: *Here it comes.*
P: I can tell! (*When Ray was physically "alive" and approached me in the dark, his energy was very strong – intense. It was not as intense now, but had the same elements and it was engulfing me.*)
R: *What would you like help with?*
P: I thought I needed help with so much, but now you're here and I'm feeling so much better. I wish you were here every minute.
R: *I am. You just don't talk to me.*

P: OK...you're right

I miss your physical presence so, Ray. I miss talking to you and hearing you...I miss hugging you. I miss your silliness.

R: *This is for the higher good and you can do this. You can do this. I know you can. We can do this. Just focus, practice and try and we can do this, baby. You did a good job tonight and we'll try again tomorrow. We'll get better and better at this and Patrick Mathews will give us validation.*

P: Okay...

What would you like me to think about or know?

R: *The Universe is a vast and wondrous macrocosm of different things, people, living beings of all types and we all must cooperate and work together to live to the fullest – reach our potentials and expand. We can do this but need people like you and others to help in whatever way you can to bring all things together in harmony and understanding...This is your work. You can do this and I will help you from this side.*

P: I love you so, angel. Always will.

R: *I love you*

April 4, 2015

P: Dear Ray – I can't stand the thought of not seeing your smile, feeling your love or having you physically here for the rest of my life. What do I do?

R: *Patricia – you will accomplish what you need to and fulfill your promises to yourself. You are at your best during difficult times. Your strength will see you through. I am RIGHT by your side and I will see you through and we will live together in eternity. Do not doubt this for one moment.*

P: All right. I'll try. I will need pep talks along the way and I need to feel your presence.

R: You will. Don't ever doubt that I love you.
P: I don't.
I love you forever.

And as always, I signed off by drawing a heart with two small hearts inside

April 11, 2015

P: Dear Ray –
I love you with all my heart. I love being able to connect with you. I wish I could feel your energy consistently. It is difficult to know you're here. Still need you to turn the candlelight on every few days so I have something visible to know you're here. I really miss seeing you.
R: *PAT! Don't do this!*
I am here next to you. I love you, my precious girl. I'm here. I haven't left you. We are one. What do I have to do or say to get you to remember that?

We are one, sweetie
We are not separate
We are together and you will be able to see me soon.
P: Ray, I need to "feel" your love somehow.
R: *Do you feel it through the writing?*
P: I do, but I'm not sure it's really you.
How do I know that it's you and not me, sweetie?
R: *I could give you a sign.*
P: Like a goat?
R: *Like a goat – an old goat (mischievous grin on his face)*
P: Ray!! (*rolling my eyes with a smirk on my face*)

OK, I'll look for a sign
R: *You've got it! I love you, precious girl.*
    Have a good night's sleep.
P: I love you, precious boy.

April 12, 2015

When I woke up this morning, the candlelight was flickering. At one point during the night – last night, I also felt this wonderful peace and this strong feeling that Ray was right by my side comforting me. Lasted 5-10 minutes.

I also saw a picture of a goat in a magazine – my sign from Ray – staring at me as if to say, "SEE!"

During those first few months and beyond, Liz and I were lonely. We cried for our unhappiness at not being able to see Ray, touch him, speak to and hear him in the traditional ways. We were deluged with fatigue – emotional and physical. It was so painful to be without his physical presence that my bones ached from the pain of separation. And yet, every night, I would ask the angels to help me to connect with Ray and every night I would be told I didn't need to ask because he was always there. Over and over he would tell me:

'We are never separate
Separate doesn't exist
Only oneness, unity
I love you
Integrate this'

But how was I supposed to know this for sure? I wanted to believe in him fully, but the doubts persisted. I was trying to be as disciplined as he wanted me to be by doing Reiki and meditating consistently to help strengthen our connection and make it clearer. I was determined to release those doubts about the oh so many signs of his presence, but my head wouldn't totally allow this to happen.

With his continued support, reinforcement and validation, however, I was beginning to move toward the idea that maybe I truly was going to be able to continue to "be" with him, but I was going to have to change my mind set. Being with him and sensing him was going to occur in a different way.

When Ray was on this plane, I perceived him – sensed him through my sight, touch, hearing, etc. – the five traditionally accepted senses. Now, perhaps, I was going to have to learn and apply a different language with a slightly different set of rules. Maybe now, I was going to be experiencing Ray in a more subtle way. Maybe now I had to learn to work within the new parameters and accept this as proof of his existence in the framework of a new reality.

Perhaps, too, our reading with Patrick Mathews scheduled to take place in a couple of weeks, would not only provide us with validation of Ray's continuing existence and his connection with us, but shed even more light on this new reality.

PHOTO 1
Ray on a family vacation in 2013.

PHOTO 2
First photo taken of Liz posing "with Ray" on Disney Bahamas cruise, July 2015.

PHOTO 3
Subsequent photo snapped within seconds of Liz's departure from photo 2. A streak of light presents itself in response to asking, "Ray, are you here?"

PHOTO 4
Light in the fireplace turns on by itself, fall 2017. Asking if Grandma Rawson and Ray are here when snapping the picture, a later viewing of the photo on the computer screen reveals two beams of light or balls of light in motion, lower left.

PHOTO 5
Subsequent photo taken seconds after photo 4 shows beams of light or balls of light in motion having traveled towards the bluish light near the door.

PHOTO 6

Winter 2016: Pointing the camera and asking, "Ray, are you here?" a very faint transparent image of Ray's face appears superimposed on the ceiling between the left wall and the first ceiling beam.

PHOTO 7
Fall 2018: In response to "Ray, are you here?" his face appears on the left in this photo taken by our spare room door.

PHOTO 8
Our spare room candlelight.

Chapter Ten

Patrick Mathews

After a great deal of anticipation, the day of our reading with Patrick Mathews had finally arrived. If all went as Liz and I hoped, we would be meeting (what would feel like) "face to face" with Ray for the first time since his passing.

Several weeks ago, I had written to Ray and asked if he could please let me know, through Patrick, if he was receiving my written communication and my love. I also wanted to know if he was traveling, had met any of our deceased relatives, and if he was, indeed, sending signals to Liz and I via feathers, birds and the light going on and off.

We were hoping for the very best, but knew there was a possibility he might not come through. Perhaps, instead, we would hear from someone else on the Other Side, who wanted or needed to give us a message and, since it was beyond our control, we knew we needed to accept that and be content. After all, that too, would be miraculous and shouldn't be minimized or unappreciated.

The Patrick Mathews' group had given us a phone number to call at precisely 9:00 am. Phones by our sides, we anxiously watched each minute pass. As the digits on the clock face rolled to the appointed time, we nervously picked up the landlines and I dialed. (Dear reader, please remember that Patrick Mathews knew absolutely nothing about me or Liz or our situation in life with or without Ray. When registering, I had only been asked to give my name, email address and payment.) Within two rings, Patrick picked up. His voice was as warm and as friendly as I had imagined when reading his books.

April 21, 2015

Notes from one hour session with Patrick Mathews

Patrick began by asking us if we had ever had a reading with him before. We told him that Liz had, but I had not. He asked with whom we wanted to connect. We told him my husband and Liz's father – Ray. Patrick told us that if we had any questions we really wanted answered to be sure to ask them up front. He didn't want us to wait until the last ten minutes of the reading, not receive an answer and be disappointed. He then said he just needed a minute. There was silence. Seemed like thirty seconds and very much to our surprise he said, "OK, got him." I took written notes, writing down word for word as much as I possibly could. Liz did the same.

Patrick: *Ray says it might surprise you but he made it to Heaven – picked the lock and squeezed through the gates.* (We all laughed. Intonation, vocabulary use, type of humor as voiced through Patrick, sounded just like Ray.)

Patrick: *I want to tell you up front how Ray passed. I'm feeling a blow to the head – did he die of a stroke?*

Pat: No, but those were the exact words the doctors used to describe what had caused his death – "blow to the head." He died from lack of oxygen to the brain.

Patrick: *Ray says his head was the thing – his brain was so big that it left no room for this to happen.* (We all chuckled.) *He wants you to know that he loves you both SO MUCH and there was nothing to be done. That was the way he was going to pass. It really was his time. He says that now he is an expert on all this "spirit stuff."* (Referring, of course, to the spiritual journey that Ray and I seemed to be on and all we had studied and learned.)

He says there is no separation between Liz and you – Pat, and him. He is there all the time. Being invisible, he can keep an eye on Liz. ☺

Pat – do you have Ray's iPhone?

Pat: Yes. (We had purchased one iPhone and I was using his.)
Patrick: Pat -- Ray says he is frustrated. He has an iPhone to the millionth and is bragging about that. He says he keeps pushing the numbers. He wants to make the phone ring for you.

He says he speaks to you every single time you speak to him.

Pat…do you have a journal? Do you write in a journal?
Pat: Yes
Patrick: *And do you write to Ray?*
Pat: (Hesitating)…Yes
Patrick: *And do you think you hear him?*
Pat: (Long pause)…Yes
Patrick: *Pat – I want to know that you **are** hearing him! You must understand that you **are** hearing! Many people think they are hearing and/or wish they could hear, but you **are** and you need to keep it up.*

*You were wondering if you were communicating/connecting with him during meditation. Journaling puts you in a meditative state and during meditation you **are** communicating. He mentions meditation in particular.*
(I was so happy I could have cried and was on the verge of tears.)

*Remember – he is **always** there, just invisible. Ray talks to Liz too. Journaling is a form of meditation. Try to get Liz to do it too.*

He wants to know if you have felt him by the side of your bed comforting you.
Pat: Yes, I have.
Patrick: *Good, because he's saying he has been there.*

Ray says he has met a lot of people. Pat – your grandfather – your Mom's Dad. He is very nice.

Ray is with your mom's mom right now and they say they are looking for someone for Liz. (Liz was not married.)

Pat – did you have two small dogs?
Pat: Yes
Patrick: *The two dogs and Ray are together. You may hear them running around the house.*

Are you going somewhere warm this summer?
Pat: Yes
Patrick: *Are you going on a cruise?*
Pat: Yes
Patrick: *Are you going to the Bahamas?*
Pat: Yes
Patrick: *Well Ray is in a tropical shirt and says he is looking forward to going too and don't let money be an object – You only live once – well, not really, but we won't go into that…* ☺

He says he will feel the sand on his feet just like you will be. He will be riding with you and walking with you and will experience things the same.

*He says **they** do the exact same things and a lot cheaper.* ☺

Again he says, don't let money be any object – live it up!

Pat – were you thinking you wanted to run a 5k or something?
Pat: (surprised) – Ray and I had talked about running – for the first time, in a 5k, a few months before he passed.
Patrick: *Well, Ray wants you to do it. He says he will be with you every step of the way. He thinks Liz should do it too.*
Pat – Ray is saying something about lights in your house. He is very happy that you are noticing the lights. He says, 'Pay attention to the lights.'
Pat – He wants you to look forward to every single day. He says he has a lot of trouble to get you into.

He also wants you to understand – don't ever question that he knows how much you and Liz love him. He hears you when you tell him – say it, think it and it is amplified a million times…as is his love to you.

Ray also wants you to keep in mind that there is nothing scary about being dead. It really is just the next phase of life.

Don't think of him as being dead – just in the next phase. He is really just invisible now. He is with you all the time, but so are all your loved ones in spirit. Probably a good thing you don't realize how much these spirits are with you – maybe you would find it bothersome. He says that when you pass into spirit, it really all makes sense.

*Again, Ray emphasizes that he really is with you **all** the time.*

He says don't be surprised if you're going to be writing a book. He is planting a seed.

He also says you've been thinking about retirement. He is biting his tongue and says he can't tell you, but you have feelings for a reason and it's up to you whether you want to give in to them.

(Patrick pauses and is quiet for a few seconds as he listens to Ray and continues…)
Patrick: Pat…………………does Ray have a tattoo?
Pat: No
Patrick: (Pauses) *No, Pat…..Ray has a tattoo*
Pat: No, he doesn't have a tattoo
Patrick: (Pauses)…*Ray says Heaven is a little more liberal* ☺

(Long pause)…*Pat, Ray has a tattoo…it's a big heart with two little hearts inside with both your names on it.*
Pat: Oh my gosh!!!
Patrick: What?

Pat: Every night –when I write in my journal – that's how I sign off – I draw a big heart with two little hearts inside labeled with our names!!

Patrick: Well, Ray says he knows. When you draw it, you are writing on his arm and it hurts. (Ray is laughing).

Pat – did you and Ray do Reiki?
Pat: Yes
Patrick: Ray says that you'd be surprised on the spirit end what is taking place while you are doing that. It is very interesting – lot more to it – lot more going on than you think.

He asks what you think of him – what you think he looks like now that he has crossed over. Do you think of him as just a ball of energy or???

He says he is still human – still a person, but in spirit. He still has two arms, two legs, and walks around and he's bragging, saying, but he can walk through walls…

*He says that there is nothing there (where you are), that is not here (where he is), but it's difficult to explain because it's like trying to explain the color blue to someone who has never seen blue before. He says that Heaven is beyond the imagination. But, he says he is a person and he emphasizes this. He says he is in the physical realm a **lot** of the time. He really is with you **all** the time. **ALL THE TIME!** He says he wants to be with you and he **is** with you…all the time. He says that if the roles were reversed and you had transitioned, where would **you** want to be. Understand that he **is here.***

*He says that he hears every word, every thought and most of all he **feels your love**. He also says he will be with you forever and that is a promise and a threat!* ☺

(Listening to Ray) Yes, Ray…that is a good way to explain it… Ray says that Heaven is all around you – it's just a different set of physics. Can he run around? Yes, but he's here with you as well.

(Pauses)

OK, Ray, he says it's like this…
*When you look at a body of water, all you can see is the top of the water, but if you stick your hand in it, there is a whole ocean underneath. This Earth – the physical – is the surface. Heaven, if we could reach our hand into it, is all around us. Ray says they (he) is able to be on top of the water and **in** the water as well. He is (and Ray interrupts) "splashing around."*

Patrick continues: *Bottom line is, according to Ray, that he wants you to know that he is STILL A PERSON and STILL WITH YOU, PERIOD! He hears every word, every thought and most of all HE FEELS YOUR LOVE.*

And I am being instructed from Ray to say this as if I mean it, HE LOVES YOU GUYS!!

He is RIGHT there. You're going to feel him and feel his presence.

Patrick: *Pat—Ray is saying, "Don't you even think about getting lazy. He will help you write your next chapter and every chapter yet to come."*

He wants to tell you not to make him work so hard …if you hear him say something, got it – go for it.
He says now that he is getting hungry and he still eats. He loves you very much and the dogs give their love too.

I was FLOORED! The reading was PHENOMENAL! **Everything** was right on the mark! I could not have dreamed of receiving anything better. All of the main questions I had asked Ray out loud or had written in my journal, prior to this reading, Patrick had answered without knowing about any of them.

In addition, I had received validation. Yes, I was hearing Ray as I wrote in the journal. Yes, Ray was turning on the light in the spare room. Yes, I did feel him by my side at night. Yes, he felt my love. He also knew what I was thinking, saying and doing. And, he would always be with us. Now, it was up to me, if I desired, to continue that connection.

That night I wrote to Ray…

April 21, 2015

Dearest Ray –

I am *so* thankful we had time together today. It was one of the best days of my life. I absolutely **loved** speaking with you. Thank you for answering so many of my questions. I was so glad that you seemed *so* happy. You well deserve it and I am *so* happy you are with Liz and me always – every step of the way.

The tattoo was cute. I'd like to get something similar, but I think I'm a little nervous about a real tattoo on this plane. Maybe a piece of jewelry – necklace? that connects us through this image?

I love you so.

(And, as always, I signed off by drawing a heart with two small hearts inside – labeled with our names.)

Chapter Eleven

Changing Perception

There are times in our lives when we are challenged with new ideas, new ways of looking at things and/or new ways of viewing the world we live in. Maybe at a head or gut level, we accept these ideas. They resonate with us. Maybe our gut or our heart tells us that these ideas – this new paradigm makes perfect sense. And yet, relinquishing old patterns of thought can be so difficult.

I knew in my heart that Ray, visible or not, was still with me. After all, he had offered validation in the form of lights, birds, feathers, connections via journaling and via Patrick Mathews. Yet my head was still clinging to old patterns of thought, doubting, and I was having trouble releasing them. It was Ray, who with love, patience and persistence held my hand and addressing my questions and doubts from the Other Side, helped to walk me through the darkness into the light.

May 10, 2015

> P: Ray, are you able to truly understand the big picture for us and why you are there, and Liz and I are here, because this arrangement is causing us a lot of pain.
> R: *Pat, I wish I could spare you any pain that you and Liz are going through right now. I love you both so much and I don't want you to be in pain, but sometimes pain is necessary for growth.*

P: You didn't have to go through this.

R: *Different strokes for different folks. You will understand when you come here, but you and Liz definitely have a purpose for being where you are at this time. It will all be understood even though everything seems to make **no** sense right now. Be patient and don't close your heart (I know you won't). I will be with you every step of the way to help guide you, support you and love you.*
Never fear, I will never leave you. I'm sorry I left the physical for you both. I know that this makes you very unhappy. I had no idea. I love you very much.

May 12, 2015

Note: No candlelight, but the phone rang twice today, then stopped. I picked up quickly but there was silence. No one was there. It was 11:40 am – the time Ray usually called from work. Was it him?

During our nightly journal conversation, we exchanged I love you's and Ray reminded me, once again, that he is always with me.

R: *I haven't left, just transitioned. I'm here. I'm holding you and I'm with you. I'm taking care of you.*
P: I know you are, in my heart.
R: *The heart tells the truth.*

May 15, 2015

P: Raymond?? Ray??
R: *Pat, I am here, as always, waiting for you. We are a family – always connected, always one, always together, never separate. Don't think of us as separate – we never could be. I love you both – you are a part of me and I, you. Talk to me. Visit with me. Walk and talk with me as*

you always would for I am here with you – just in a different form. A form you will be in soon. Do not be afraid that I am not here, because that will never happen.

Love. Trust. Believe.

This is a truer reality than the reality in which you live now. Don't be afraid. The Universe opens its loving arms to help and guide you.

Try this: Say my name 3x.
Now breathe and count to 3.
Think of me and pretend you are opening your heart to my love.

I love you.

P: I love you.

May 17, 2015

Dear angels,
    May I please speak to Ray?
P: Raymond??
R: I'm here, precious girl.
P: Oh sweetie – I need you.
R: I'm right here – right next to you and I won't leave 'til you're ready. Don't be afraid. I'm here to comfort, love you and take care of you.
P: I love you so.
R: Remember, love never dies and we are bonded like super glue. ☺ Nothing can tear us apart –nothing. I haven't left and you need to trust that and work with that. I am always at your side. If you want extra love, I am here. Strength, I am here. Confidence, I am here. Guidance, I am here. I am here. I am here, Pat. I am here and when

*you talk of doing things for the first time without me, remember that you are just talking about **your** version of "3D." But I **am** here and I **am** with you.*

P: I loved you in "3D" and it gave me such joy. Holding your hand and having you beside me sent me to cloud nine. I need to feel your love in my heart. Can we work on that?

R: *Of course we can. I love you, Pat. Please try to remember this and try **hard**. I **am** here.*

Again, later that day, May 17, 2015

P: Raymond?? Raymond??
Sweetie, I'm having a sad day today. I miss you. Please help me.

R: *Patricia, I am with you.*
Hold out your hand…
Take three deep breaths…
Can you feel the warmth around your hand?

P: Yes, I think I can.

R: *I am here. I told you and keep telling you.*
I am here. Try to relax, believe and trust.
I am here, Say it at least 10x each day.

Ray is here and he loves me.
Ray is here and he loves me.

You can do this, Pat. You can do this and it won't be long 'til we're together again and this time for eternity. You can do this, sweetie. Trust. Believe and Root Yourself in this Belief.

P: Oh sweetie, I'll try. Thank you.

(And it was AMAZING how that "Ray is here…" mantra helped!)

May 18, 2015

>Dear angels,
> May I please speak to Ray?
>
>P: Raymond? Raymond?
>R: *(lovingly)* *I tell you all the time. I am right here. You're making me work very hard on this. I love you, sweetie. You're a fast learner, but you're being slow on this. I am here. Say: Ray is here and he loves me.*
>P: (I repeat 3x)
>R: *That's it. I love you.*
>P: I love you so much.
>R: *I know you do. I am here beside you.*

May 19, 2015

>P: Ray?? What do you want me to know?
>R: *Never doubt how much I love you or how much I am here for you. I am and so are many others. Don't forget your angels and guides are ready to help you through this as well. We are here for you. You may not be able to see us, but you can't see electricity or lots of other things and they are there. We are too. We love you and will take care of you. We're a powerful force and don't underestimate because we are out of sight.*
>P: I love you.
>R: *I love you too.*

May 20, 2015

>Dear angels,
> May I please speak to Ray?
> Raymond? Raymond?

R: *Patricia. I love you with all my heart and soul…and don't forget it.*
P: You are my soul – so much of who I am. I can't bear losing "me." We are one. You are me. I am you.
R: *Pat, you have to realize that we are closer now than ever before. You don't see me, but energetically there is no separation, sweetheart. None. Love is energy. Energy transcends all. I have transcended all and I am with you.*

May 27, 2015

Dear angels,
   May I please speak to Ray?

P: Raymond – sweetie – are you there?
R: *Patricia – you know I am. I love you.*
P: I love you, sweetie. It is very difficult getting used to this way of communicating with you.
R: *Why? You often said you were talking to my behind or I wasn't in the room and you got upset.* ☺
P: (smiling) OK….maybe so.
R: *So, think of it as I was training you for this time and these moments. Pretty good, huh? I was on the ball.* ☺
P: Yes, we know. ☺

May 31, 2015

P: Raymond, are you there?
R: *Of course I'm here. You don't even need to ask. I am always waiting for you my precious girl. Why would I not come to you if you call me? It's not like on the Earth plane.* ☺ *You speak and I hear every word, thought. We are one and it feels so good. I wish I could explain. You are the Universe. I am the Universe. We are all things. The whole is*

never separate from its parts. We are all one. We learn separateness on your plane for survival, but that is not how it really is. You need to say "I love you" because of this separateness that we are taught, but I feel your love and I will teach you to feel mine.

P: I love you so much.
R: *I know and (whispering)... I..........................*
Loveeee.............................
Youuuuuuuu..........................

June 6, 2015

P: Raymond, sweetie, are you there?
R: *I'm always here for you. I told you that.*
P: I am so sorry for not always knowing how to do better by you when you were here.
R: *Pat – we all have our ups and downs. We are all learning. You are not to blame and don't blame yourself. All is well. It's all about learning and returning home. No need to fret, regret, be hard on yourself. All our brains get clouded. If you want forgiveness, I will forgive you but only if you forgive me – which I know you have and we always voiced and exchanged this while on the Earth plane together.*

All truly is well

Pat – I love you. Don't ever think that I don't. Just because you can't see me doesn't mean I'm not real. I am and I am talking to you. It will get stronger. My love for you will only grow.

P: I love you with all my heart.

June 13, 2015

Dear angels,
   May I please speak to Ray?

P: Raymond?
R: Pat, I'm here. You are so sweet. I love to have you write to me each night. It means so much to me and I love to connect with you. Other people hope for that too – with their loved ones. I know you are learning to communicate more efficiently and we are all very excited! (Tell Liz how proud I am of her.)
   Pat – please know how much I love you and intend to take care of you and look after you. You are well cared for so don't be afraid to do things you've always dreamed of.

June 24, 2015

P: Ray?
R: Pat, I'm here. It is kind of fun being invisible.
P: For you, yes, for us – we can't see you!
R: Why do you have to see me?
P: I liked looking at your eyes – especially the way they would look at me to tell me you loved me and that someone on this crazy plane really cared about me and thought I was special. I miss that – the sparkle in your eye, the grin on your face, the little dance you would do when you were excited. All of the things that enriched my life so…
R: Do you think we could work on other ways to enrich your life and the lives of others?
P: We could.

June 25, 2015

Yesterday I asked for a sign that Ray was around. Today I found a beautiful hawk feather in the pool area. Hawks were Ray's favorite birds.

June 27, 2015

A few nights ago, around 1:00 am, while sleeping, I awoke to a bird furiously pecking at my window screen. Scared me. Have never had a bird do that before, and to my knowledge, birds don't typically do that. Seemed very persistent, as if he desperately wanted my attention. It was difficult to make out what type of bird it was, in the dark, but from what I could discern, it seemed to be a medium-sized bird – dark – kind of looked like Gordon, the crow I see in the morning.

Today, during the day, I saw another bird clinging to the same screen. I can't remember ever having seen a bird cling to our window screens during all the years we've been in the house except for the one mentioned above. I asked if it was a sign from Ray. The bird stayed for a moment and flew away.

June 29, 2015

Phone rang today about 11:45 this morning – around the time Ray used to call from work. I picked up and no one was there.

Dear angels,
    May I please speak to Ray?

R: *You know I'm here for you.*
P: I know you are. Thank you, sweetie. Thank you so much. I'm so glad I have you in at least *some* form.
R: *It's a better form – the new and improved me.* ☺

July 3, 2015

Last night, at 11:00 pm, what looked to be the same type of bird as before – Gordon? – returned pecking at my bedroom window screen. There is now a quarter sized hole in the screen. Tonight at 3:00 am, not being able to sleep, I went into the kitchen to make a cup of tea. The bird returned once again, to the kitchen window screen and resumed his relentless pecking. I opened the blinds. The bird looked me in the eye and then flew away. Could Ray just be trying to tell me he is here with me wherever I am?

July 4, 2015
Morning

I am writing to Ray about feeling lonely. I am very upset he left me so abruptly. He said we would go together (although I knew that was highly unlikely). He felt a pain and kept exercising **through** it! He apologizes while I was writing this and says he really thought it was a pulled ligament. My response:

P: I know Ray. I really do. It's just that now you are gone from me. What do I do now?
R: *I am here for you. I love you. I will help you and talk to you. I can make things easier for you. I can comfort you. I love you. What is love? Love is that magical energetic connection between two people and we have that. I can teach you to connect with me on a different level. We won't have our Earth relationship but we can have another and it will be beautiful. I truly love you.*
P: I know you do and I hope you know how very much I love you.
R: *I do and we can work this out. You'll see. Now go feed the birds you wanted to. Then come up and do Reiki. All the while say, "Raymond is here and he loves me."*
P: I love you.
R: *(whispering) I……………Love………………Youuuuu………..*

July 6, 2015

Dear angels,
    May I please speak to Ray?

R: *I'm here. I've been waiting for you. I look forward to our being together.*

P: I love you! What would you like me to know today, sweetie?

R: *Pat, the Earth is comprised of so many facets that are all interwoven to create the circumstances, situations, people and their characteristics, timing and events that need to occur so that people can complete their journeys. You are **one** segment of the whole, just as I was. You will change and the events, etc., around you will change.*

    Pat – you, Liz and when I was on that plane are all very important pieces of the grand puzzle, just as everyone is. Picture that in order for a complete picture to evolve, all the pieces need to fit together perfectly and God does that – takes you and me and Liz and everyone and fits all the pieces together for the greater whole – the greater good.

P: But now you're on the Other Side – who takes or becomes your piece? I liked – I loved – I needed your puzzle piece.

R: *Pat – Your piece will grow and contort to be mine and the picture – the overall picture can and will change so that there is an even more beautiful picture. New pieces will be needed and old ones will evolve. All for the greater good.*

    Pat, Pat. I'm here and we are still one – still one. You can't get rid of me that easily. Remember, perception needs to be changed. Seeing is not the primary sense.

P: What is?

R: *Love and not seeing with your eyes....think of the "clairs" (clairaudience, clairsentience, etc.). I'm with you, Pat. Trust, Believe, you will see.*

July 10, 2015

P: Raymond?

R: I'm here as I always am.

P: I love you.

R: I know you do, Pat and that's why I'm here.

P: Yes…

R: I want to tell you a story. A story about a cute little girl named Patty, who sat on a rock and waited and waited for her husband to return, but he didn't – not in the form she wanted him to, but in a different, more magnificent version of what he was before. She wept because she could not see him with her eyes, but she could hear him. Would she rather have **seen** him but not **heard** him?

P: No

R: Sweetie – I am here. You can hear me and you will be able to feel me. You have certainly been doing this. I am here. Enjoy the "we" we have until this phase passes and you and Liz and I are together for all eternity. I am ready to begin a new segment of our journey together. This is quite an adventure. I hope you are as excited as I am.

P: Don't forget me!

R: There's the doubting.
NO MORE PAT
NO MORE

P: OK… I love you…I am definitely in and eager to connect in the best way possible with you.

R: *(whispering)* I………………………
        Loveee………………
        Youuuuuuu………………

Chapter Twelve
A New Adventure

So Ray was "alive." He was with me. I didn't feel as though I could always access him when I wanted, but he was definitely around me and definitely making his presence known. Now, if I wanted to continue a "relationship," I had to learn to connect with him, comfortably, in this new form. And in some ways, as he had mentioned before, it *was* a more magnificent form – a purely beautiful form.

 I shared the fact that I was journaling with a few close friends. Their response would often include a question as to what Ray was like when I heard him. I would respond in this way: think about a person in your life – a family member or anyone you care deeply about. We all have our ups and downs – great parts of our personality and then problem areas. Relationships with anyone can be wonderful, but also trying at times. In our relationships with these people, though, there are times when they may say or do something that touches your heart so deeply it leaves you speechless or brings you to tears. You are connected heart to heart. You are witnessing the most beautiful part of them – glimpsing their soul. You stand in awe and fall in love with them, even more deeply. This is who Ray was now – all the time—the Ray I wrote to each night. This is the Ray whose hand I wanted to grasp as we began a new segment of our journey together. (Yes, I was still hurting) but having had a life full of adventures; maybe this was going to be our greatest adventure yet.

A New Adventure

July 14, 2015

P: Ray, I love you. Is there anything you would like to tell me today – right now?

R: *Pat, it is time for you to move to another phase and appreciate what we had, but to focus on the now and build our present relationship – enter a new phase. We can have a very strong, fulfilling relationship as we both interact with our higher selves. I love you so much. I know you love me so much. We can do this and maybe help others to do the same, if they wish. Are you ready for this part of the journey?*

P: I am so ready for anything that brings me closer to you. I love you.

Ray, why did you have to leave us when you did?

R: *Pat, it was my time. We three are on this journey together – to help each other, to see each other through. We all have a part so our souls can progress and we made a pact on the Other Side to do it this way. You just don't remember. We will be together soon. I promise. I haven't left. As I've said before, I'm with you, working with you, loving you, talking to you. Nothing has changed except I am my best self and I know not seeing me gives you distress. The more work you do now, the more connected we will be until the ultimate connection soon. Does this make any sense to you?*

P: It does. I want to strengthen our bond. I adore you – always have – always will.

July 16, 2015

P: Dear angels,
May I please speak to Ray?

Ray?? Raymond?? Raymond??
Sweetie, I love you.

R: *I know. I love you. Remember, we're not apart. I'm right here next to you, looking over your shoulder to see what you're writing.*

P: Ray, as you know, we're going to Disney World next week and on a cruise. Patrick Mathews said you're going with us and I am SO happy. So is Liz, but we can't see and feel you, so it will be very difficult for us.
How will we know you're there and beside us? I'm afraid to go… We just want you with us.

R: *Sweetheart, I **will** be there with both of you. I **will**. I promise. Don't think that because you cannot see me, I'm not there. There you go again. Seeing is just one sense. There are others.*

P: I can't *feel* you physically here…*smell* you…

R: *Those are more earthly. You have more refined senses like clairaudience, sentience, etc. You are very well aware of these and you and Liz need to use these! Think of yourself as babies learning to use your senses. You can do this. I will lead you through. I will try to give as many signs as possible.*

P: OK….It's what we have.

R: *Remember – we're on a mission – "a journey," the three of us. We have a job to do, and this is how we agreed to do it. Love transcends all boundaries. I will be wrapping you both in my love and I know you will be wrapping me in yours. We can do this!!*
Please understand that I know this is difficult. But we are the only ones who can give this piece. We can do this!

P: OK, sweetie. I will give this a good try.

July 17, 2015

Dear angels,
May I please speak to Ray?

Ray?? Raymond?

R: *Pat…you need to know and trust that I'm here every minute of every day – right by your side. I love you. I'm always there for Liz too. Am excited about the cruise. We'll all have a great time…I'm so sorry you're sad, but I **am** here. I promise.*

P: What did you do today?

R: *I'm working on improving communication. How am I doing?*

P: Ray, you've been AMAZING – lights going on and off and phones ringing, speaking to me every night…FABULOUS, FABULOUS, OVER THE TOP, GREAT JOB! OUTSTANDING! No one could be better!

R: *I love you. I am so happy I can make you happy. I will be with you on vacation – EVERYWHERE, REMEMBER!*

P: I love you!

July 18, 2015

P: Ray?? What would you like to share with me today, honey?

R: *I want to continue to connect with you and keep making that connection stronger, but I need you to raise your vibration to me. So, I need you to do Reiki and meditation, anything spiritual and to think as many positive thoughts as you can. All of these things will help. Even though I know it is extremely hard, you are capable of connecting with me in ways you would have thought impossible.*
I know it is a long road to travel before we all acknowledge all of this, but the road is coming to an end – when all people will be able to connect.
I will be helping you to reach further.

P: I love you.

(And as always, I signed off by drawing a heart, with two small hearts inside.)

Chapter Thirteen

Stepping Outside the Box

Ray had informed Liz and me via journaling and Patrick Mathews that he would be with us during our first vacation "without" him. The week before our vacation, Liz and I had attended a class at a local healing center. A quote on the classroom wall caught our attention: "We are here by faith, not by sight." I scribbled the quote in my notebook and revisited those notes, now, the day before our trip. In the evening, I wrote to Ray:

July 21, 2015

    P: Dear Ray –
         We are headed to Disney tomorrow. We're afraid to confront Disney without you. For you, Liz and I – it was *our* place! You will be with us for sure, right?

    R: *I will be with you for sure. Don't doubt. You looked at the quote on the classroom wall for a reason – as a reminder – "We are here by faith, not by sight."*

         Remember!

July 22, 2015

    Today we flew to Orlando. Ray, Liz and I always traveled together. We would sit together occupying three seats on one side of the plane. As a result, we never had an empty seat next to us, and when we would look around the plane on a flight to Orlando, no empty seats would be available. Today, Liz and I chose a middle and aisle seat on the right side of the plane. One seat, by the window, was then left to be occupied. The plane was full, but much to our surprise, no one ever asked about or took that remaining seat – the seat next to us that Ray would normally have taken. We stared at each other in disbelief, then giggled. We guessed it was Ray's seat. Was he traveling with us?

    After we checked into our hotel at Disney and began to get ready for bed, the lights suddenly flickered – on then off, in the bedroom. That had never happened before on any of our Disney trips – an electrical glitch…or Ray?

July 23, 2015

    Liz and I knew that entering the park for the first time, without Ray, would be very difficult. All kinds of memories would surface, and right now memories were painful. They reminded us he wasn't there. Taking all of this into consideration, we decided to set our bar low and see if we could just wade into the Magic Kingdom by entering the main gate and walking down Main Street without crying. This would be our first step and pave the way for future visits.

    Well, we accomplished our task! We were very proud of ourselves and felt Ray would have been proud of us too! He said he would be with us, so playing along, I didn't mention anything about the parks in my evening journal entry. I just allowed him to take the lead and discuss what he felt was important for the day. His message:

    R: *Pat, I'm here. I love you and please tell Liz I love her.*

> *I don't like to discuss this, but it will soon be a little more difficult to communicate with me as I will be in a different phase. Will you still be able to do it? Of course you will. Keep doing what you are doing. Do your Reiki, meditate, and continue to write. The more you do, the stronger our connection grows.*

P: I'm nervous, Ray.

R: *You won't lose contact. I promise. It's just a little more difficult, but you and Liz will be able to surmount all obstacles. Don't worry. I'll still be there all the time. All will be fine. I probably shouldn't have said anything.*

P: Thanks for saying something anyway. I love you so much.

R: *I love **you** so much.*

July 24, 2015

Liz and I were continuing our "vacation" by embarking on a short Disney cruise to the Bahamas with Ray's sisters. Liz and I shared a room. Our two names, as occupants, were posted by the door to our room. We laughed as soon as we opened the door and looked around because there were three sets of everything – towels, etc., as if three people were staying in the room, when the staff *knew* it was just two! Throughout the cruise, our room steward continued to leave three sets of everything – bedtime chocolates, pirate night scarves, etc. Definitely **not** something that typically happened…Ray???

In the evening, when I wrote, Ray said that he was glad the trip was working out. He knew it would and knew that his sister, Jan, would be so excited. He continued by saying that he enjoyed dinner with us and added:

> R: *I can't tell you how much it means to me when I see you happy and laughing. I want this for you and Liz. I am happy here, although I miss you.*

July 21, 2015

Before Ray transitioned, he, Liz and I enjoyed traveling and had taken several cruises. One of our rituals was to walk a mile – doing laps around the ship, after dinner. Honoring that tradition, Liz and I decided to walk the mile, alone, for the first time.

Not too long into the walk, we paused by a section of the ship's railing, as we usually did with Ray, so I could take a photo of Ray and Liz. This time, without Ray physically present, I asked Liz if maybe she could stand by the railing and position her arm to "include her father." (Photo 2) She agreed, and then after posing for several photos, resumed walking. I stayed behind for a moment, pointed the camera to the same spot and whispered, "Ray, are you here?" I then snapped three photos in quick succession. On returning home and looking at the photos on the computer screen, I noticed a beam of light streaking through one of those photos. I had read and heard on several occasions, from researchers, that this streak of light could definitely be a sign of a departed loved one's presence. (Photo 3)

Throughout our vacation, in addition to the aforementioned signs, we heard Ray's favorite song played in public places more than once. We also saw a newly released movie onboard the cruise ship in which his favorite quote played a central role. We certainly felt as though Ray had indeed accompanied us on vacation.

On returning home I wrote:

July 29, 2015

P: Raymond?
R: *Did you like the vacation?*

P: I did, sweetie. You really were there. It was difficult, at times, because we couldn't see you with our eyes. We sensed you a lot. Loved that the room steward on the cruise kept delivering three chocolates, three of everything, when the room was registered for two people.

Did you feel a part of everything?

R: *Pat, I want you to know how much I love you and Liz and yes, I did feel part of everything. You are a wonder…I had a great time with you. You made me feel part of your experience. I loved it. I was very proud of you.*

I love the tattoo, by the way. Now we're twins!

P: We are! It's to be another connection between the two of us! :)
(*I had gotten a henna tattoo at Disney – a big heart with two little hearts inside.*)

I want to get a locket or bracelet – a simple, beautiful locket or bracelet, so that I have a visual of your being with us all the time. I thought it might help.

R: *Pat, I will see what I can do to find one for you. Your wish is my command. Never forget how much I love you.*

P: And how much I love you – how very much I love you. You have been unbelievable! You have been trying **so** hard to be with us, talk to us, and show us you're here. We are speechless! Don't know what to say that begins to express how extremely appreciative we are. Thank you. Thank you. Thank you.

And as always, I signed my nightly journal entry by drawing a heart with two small hearts inside, labeled with our names.

Chapter Fourteen

Forging Ahead

Six months and counting. So much had transpired since Ray's passing – so much to learn, so many obstacles to surmount. Yet it really felt as though Ray was trying to help us through these difficult times by holding our hands and guiding us as best he could. He really seemed to be going to extraordinary lengths to communicate and tell us he was beside us, lending his support. He wanted us to know he was still our foundation. And if I believed this was so, how could I let him down by not matching his effort? I realized I had to step up to the plate and try my best to strengthen our connection so we could play out the potential of this adventure.

July 31, 2015

> P: Raymond? Ray? I love you.
> R: *I love you.*
> P: Ray – what would you like to share with me today? Would love to know how best to connect with you.
> R: *Pat – It is **so** simple. Open your heart and mind and let me in. There is nothing fancy or complicated. No magic. You are a child of God and as such have the ability to do all kinds of things. Speaking to someone on the Other Side is as easy as speaking to someone here on this plane. Just need to listen – focus and listen – redirect your thoughts to your inner self rather than outer self. Listen to the small voice within*

*which can be found during quiet, tranquil times and meditation. Expect that this will happen, but know that it can take practice. You know how to do this and you **can** do this.*

Our love is the energy that binds – that connects us together. It is the telephone wire – the conduit. It works. You just have to set it up and listen. Clearer transmission and reception comes from everyday practice and belief.

P: Thank you, sweetie. I love you so!!

August 1, 2015

P: Ray??
R: *I'm here as I always am.*
P: How should I meditate best – just by focusing on breathing?
R: *You can focus on breathing, a question you want answered or just peace or a mantra…*

Stay positive, meditate, do Reiki. You're getting there.
P: Why do I need to "stay positive?"
R: *Staying positive is essential for manifesting… The high energy carries the good vibration.*
P: I love you.

August 2, 2015

P: Dear angels,
May I please speak to Ray?

Raymond? Raymond? Raymond?
R: *Pat, I'm here for you, babe.*
P: Ray, I get so disheartened. It is so difficult here. I am just so tired. My stomach hurts. I'm hungry.

R: Pat – give yourself a break – take a breath and do something different than you normally do. You need rest. You've had a lot thrown on you with me, the house and with Liz. You're tired. You're exhausted. You need rest and a break and the whole world will seem better. You did well to meditate.
P: I love you, Raymond.

August 3, 2015

P: Raymond? Raymond?
R: *Pat, you're crying.*
P: Angel, I need you and miss your being physically here.
R: *I know you found my heart.*
P: (Ray used to give me hearts. Once it was a porcelain heart. Often they were different types of small stone hearts. Once or twice they were heart ornaments for Christmas. This time it was a clear crystal stone heart that I found in a small gift box on one of the shelves in Ray's bedroom closet. The box was on a shelf where he would hide Christmas or birthday presents for me).
P: I did, sweetie, did you mean it for me?
R: *Yes, but you had so many.*
P: I *love* it!
R: *Pat – clear you mind and emotions. Now listen:*
The most beautiful part of a marriage is the energetic connection that two people make – that spark that ignites when you meet – some people call it chemistry and that stays throughout the relationship. We had this for 40+ years on the Earth plane, but we STILL have it. That energetic connection never dies – the pilot light never goes out – it is always STILL THERE.
I love you and always will. My love never dies, just as yours for me never dies or mine for Liz or hers for me.
Remember this. Integrate this. As for the clear heart, you needed love

today and this is for you. It will help you during your difficult times. Cleanse it and use it when you write to me. I love you, sweetheart.

P: Ray, I love you with all my heart.

R: *I know. You'll be OK. You'll see.*

August 4, 2015

P: Ray, I love you and miss your being physically here… I don't think I can do this. There is such a huge hole inside me.

R: *… Pat, I'm not going to tell you that all of this you're going through is easy. There is a lot of pain and suffering and I wish I could take it from you, but I can't. You will come to terms, however, and all will be palatable. I will be here for you, helping you, supporting you, connecting with you. You have nothing to fear and before you know it, we'll all be together again. I promise it won't be long.*

Our life force is one.

Ray, Liz and I lived about an hour from the shore. During the summer, we used to love to pack a picnic dinner and drive down to the beach after work. We'd have dinner overlooking the Sound and then walk the beach and watch the sun set. It was very special to us, and Liz and I were very nervous about doing this for the first time without Ray.

August 7, 2015

Journal entry:

Went to the shore today with Liz. Liz brought sandwiches for dinner and the plan was to picnic at a pavilion and then walk the beach. We were a little nervous (a lot nervous) going without Ray physically here. We began the walk at Meigs Point. It was difficult to hold back the tears, but we did. At one point we just sat on one of the large boulders and held each other.

We then decided to walk the length of the beach – the route we always took as a family, wading into the water, up to our ankles, along the way. Not too long into the walk, we began to notice seagull feathers along the path, on the sand, one here…then another…then another… Made me think of bread crumbs lining the path for Hansel and Gretel. Never experienced anything like this before. At final count there were fifty-six feathers altogether, joining us on our walk! Ray was always collecting feathers.

Ray was definitely with us! Thank you from the bottom of our hearts, Ray!

When I wrote to Ray that night:

P: Raymond?
R: *Patricia, I'm here.* ☺
   *Never fear because I am **always** with you.*
P: Ray – Liz and I couldn't believe the number of feathers you placed on the beach so we'd know you were with us. We were so comforted and it felt *so* good – in ecstasy to know you were and are with us.
R: *What have I told you? Trust I am with you always. You are my girls. I love you. (Pat begins to cry)*
   …It's OK. Tears cleanse the soul, but you know there's no need since I'm right here. I'm not worried about you as I, more than anyone, know your strength and that in time, you will do very well. Don't worry. We won't lose sight of each other – just the physical pain will subside. Then the best part of our relationship begins. ☺ *I love you, my sweetheart.*
P: I love YOU!

August 13, 2015

P: Ray – thank you so much for always being here, honey. Thank you for giving me signs like one of your favorite songs – "Greensleeves"—as I walked upstairs and turned on the TV today. You can see *me* seeing *your* signs, but I can't tell if you feel or receive *my* love. I want you to feel it or know that I am sending it to you. How would I know? (Even though Patrick Mathews told me you do, but…)

R: *Pat – It is said that our hearts are meant to love and love they do. The love given to another jumps across an energy bridge to that other person. We feel it. I feel it.*
How do you explain that "love" feeling? Is it warmth? Tingling? A feeling of joy? Satisfaction? Peace? Exhilaration? You can have these feelings to know it is returned.
Do you have any of these feelings when you kythe or meditate with me?

P: Yes, I do.

R: *Then it is returned.*

P: But even though I might get some of those feelings, that doesn't necessarily mean they are from you – could just be me? It is through the look in someone's eyes and their actions that I can tell.

R: *You do not have the look in my eyes, but feathers, my notes, lights, "Greensleeves," etc. Doesn't that tell you?*

P: Yes, it does. I love you.

August 18, 2015

P: Dear Ray –
Last night – well all yesterday, as you know, I cried most of the day. I was cleaning the spare room and bookshelf upstairs. I

Forging Ahead

would run across things important to you or both of us and miss your physical presence so.

R: *It will get better. I know the pain is unbearable. We will get you through this and…if it had been me in your spot, I wouldn't have done any better – maybe worse. You have people who love you on this side and that, just as I do…*

P: I spoke to you all day. At one point I heard you say that I was doing it again – living in the past or what might have been, instead of what is and that I had to grab hold of what is, plunge myself into this part of the journey or adventure and run with it so that I could connect in the best possible way with you, if that is what I want.
I want to be able to sense your love. It is important to me and I know it would be important to others to be able to experience this with their deceased loved ones.

R: *Meditation is the key. Pat, it is so important for you to meditate every day if you wish to connect with me at a higher level and greater degree. We need to match vibrations which we can easily do if you meditate. So just as you focus on writing to me, focus on this as well. When you are able to relax, we will meditate together. You will learn to feel my love in a different way. You already have and I'm proud of you for this – the feathers, etc.*
Pat – we will be together – so soon!!! When it finally happens you will laugh about how short this part of the journey was.

P: I love you so very much.

R: *I love you so much.*

Chapter Fifteen
Finding Joy

Liz and I were attempting to forge a pass through what seemed like a mountain of grief. Sometimes, however, it felt like such a formidable task. I know there were times when I felt like I was making great strides. Then, I'd fall back into a stream of sadness and tears. The grief counselor had warned that this would happen – depression coming in waves and it certainly did.

Someone once said, "The more you love, the more you hurt." In one of Ray's messages, he said, "You are human and so you love. Don't feel ashamed of your behavior…it all takes time." So, placing one foot in front of the other, I persevered. Liz and I both persevered as Ray, ever present, offered wisdom and support. He wanted to help us discover that path to happiness and embrace joy to the highest degree possible. Liz and I wanted and needed to find joy, even though it seemed elusive.

August 23, 2015

    P: Raymond?
    R: *I'm here. I'm always here, sweetheart.*
    P: I love you. So much of me won't believe you're not here anymore.
    R: *That's because I **am** here and inside you realize this and fully accept it. It is the so-called "rational" brain that refuses or is hesitant to accept "the truth." I **am** with you all the time – in a different*

guise, but here and I am here to help you and Liz and comfort you and Liz and go on adventures and enjoy everything you enjoy right alongside you.

August 24, 2015

R: *Pat, I wish you would or could completely understand how I am with you all the time, so that you would not fret or even feel lonely or upset. I am next to you every second of every day. There is never a moment when I am not with you. One day you will understand, but I wish it was now to alleviate any heartache.*

P: You have said I will be "without" you for only a speck of time, but I can't see you.

R: *Would you rather **see** but not **hear** me?*

P: No, I'm extremely happy to hear you.

August 25, 2015

R: *I wish I knew how to help you even more than I am.*

P: Sweetheart – I know you love me and loving someone means trying any way to make them happy. I know this of you – that you are trying to the nth degree and I thank you.

R: *Pat – I know how difficult it can be on your plane. There is so much turmoil – man-made and other, but we need to remember, that in the midst of darkness, there is light and a reason for all, even though there might not seem like any. We all have a reason for being and for real – a reason for "dying" or passing over. Remember, as I said before, that we are all pieces of a puzzle. Every single one of us is unique and beautiful and lends a beauty to the whole that **not one** other person on this Earth can contribute. Own the beautiful piece that you are and celebrate it, embrace it and use it to shed light and bring even more beauty to the entire whole.*

P: I think it is truly beautiful what you are saying, it's just that – what seems to make life beautiful is the joy we share with our loved ones. When our loved ones pass, so does joy.

R: *You give us too much credit. We do create joy, but joy can be created in so many ways.*

P: You and Liz are my joy. I love you SO much.

R: *We adore you too, my sweetheart, but you shouldn't put your light out just because the food for your light has been diminished. You need to find an additional source, so your God-given light will shine bright again.*

P: But why?

R: *It's why you came to this plane. We all have a job to do – work to be done – lessons to learn and helping others with their lessons. None of these can happen if we shut ourselves in a closet.*

P: Then I will need LOTS of help – especially from you. I will need strength from you.

August 26, 2015

P: Sweetie – It is my understanding that the more positive I am, the easier it is for you to communicate with me, but I miss your physical presence. This has been very traumatic. How am I supposed to be happy and positive?

R: *It is complex, but I think that all the right answers are at our fingertips. You need to relax first. You are tired, overwhelmed and taking on too much. You and Liz need to do exactly what* **truly** *makes you happy – not what you* **think** *will make* **other** *people happy – not right now anyway. This is how you will put the joy in your heart.*

Think about what really makes your heart sing – what excites you – what makes you giggle—what makes you laugh—what gives you inside satisfaction – what touches your heart. These are the things that truly give you joy and **this** *is what you need to do.*

> *Think carefully because you might say that doing something for someone else gives joy and it does and can, but you need things that don't require a lot of work – emotionally and physically but make you happy. Here lies the answer. I truly love you both. Focus on this now. Meditate and sit in the power as you were told. Our connections will be even stronger and even more joy will result.*

August 27, 2015

> R: Pat, never forget how precious you are to me and I don't want Liz to forget how precious she is to me.…Just because you can't see me, doesn't mean I don't think about you and love you all the time. I'm also with you all the time.
> Remember, you can't see me, but you still love me. I love **you**!

September 1, 2015

> P: Raymond?? Raymond??
> R: Pat, I'm here every second.
> P: Sweetie, I look at your picture and see my joy – my joy in another dimension.
> R: Pat, you must focus on the now and the future…
> P: I will try.
> R: Focus on what you **can** do. Then the world becomes an open book.

September 2, 2015

Journal entry:

I was feeling pretty blue today, missing Ray and all that is and was. Early in the morning, after I got out of bed, I was upstairs, looking out the window and I saw a hawk land and stare at me from the top of our swing set. Had never seen that before, (Ray?)

Tonight, I was in the spare room, answering emails and just as I finished – around 10:00, the candlelight in the room started flickering. Then it stopped and just remained on. It hasn't been on since April!! Not at all!!

Thank you so very, very much, Ray! I………………………… Loveeee……………Youuuuu….

Dear angels,
May I please speak to Ray?

Raymond???

R: *You know I'm here!*

P: I am so happy and so excited. I feel invigorated and excited. I feel hopeful!

R: *Pat, know that I'm here always. Even when the candle light isn't on. I am with you – every second –**all the time**!*

P: Thank you Ray. Thank you for the signs today – especially the light. I *really* needed it! What would you like me to know, sweetie?

R: *Just pause for a minute and think of the most beautiful thing you can think of…*

P: That's easy – you, Liz and I sitting on the rocks at Acadia on top of Cadillac mountain. You have your arms around me and you are kissing the top of my head. Liz is with us and we are hugging her too. My most joyful dream time – all of us together.

R: *Now hold onto that for a minute.*

P: What do you want me to do now?

R: *I think that you think that joy is fleeting, but that joy which you keep in your memory and in your heart is inside you all the time, waiting to be brought to the surface. Bring it to the surface whenever you need to.*

P: But I don't have that joy perceived by my senses in real time – in the here and now.
R: *What did I hear you say to someone once? Adjustments have to be made? Things don't stay the same. They are in constant flux. This is the way life is.*
P: OK, got me. I don't really like change. I love you so much, Raymond Overton.
R: *I love you.*

September 3, 2015

Journal entry: The light in the spare room, that had come on yesterday, went off by itself around 8:00 am. I had been in the room earlier, left, and when I returned it had turned itself off. I cannot even begin, as I write this tonight, to convey the amount of pain that I feel missing Ray. He will repeatedly say, "I am here." He shows me with the light etc. that he is. I love him. I miss seeing him. It hurts.

P: Ray – I'm upset because I miss your physical presence – your smile, laugh, the twinkle in your eyes when you look at me, your kiss on my forehead…
R: *Do you remember how they felt?*
P: Yes
R: *You have them. You have the memory of what it feels like and looks like. You're tired. Sleep!*

September 4, 2015

P: Raymond Overton, Jr…I love you so much! ☺
Is there anything you'd like to share with me today?
R: *Pat, I'm holding you right now. If you meditate – when you meditate, you would feel things more strongly. You will enjoy that.*

Pat – I treasure you and our time together and we will have so much more time together – you just wait and see. Don't lose hope. Don't be sad. This is just the beginning of another one of our adventures – more exciting than all of the others put together. You will walk with me, talk with me, just as you always did, but this time it will be even better.

These are the thoughts you need to hold onto and run with – not the sadness of the old, but the excitement of the new.

I am with you always. With a smile on your face, trust, believe, hold my hands and meditate and let's explore a new world together. "Raymond is here and he loves you" and wants to be with you and don't doubt or forget it!

September 5, 2015

P: Ray, what would you like to share with me?

R: *Pat, I wish I could tell you everything. I know, as a learner, you are interested in everything. Some things you just have to experience because there are no words to describe it. My world is filled with brilliant wonder, peace, love and camaraderie…*

On the Earth plane, there is huge greed, selfishness, etc. Those traits must be on the Earth plane to learn. If it was the same as Heaven, how could you ever learn?

P: Ray, I don't understand why there had to be *so* much pain, sometimes, on this side.

R: *Pat, it's very complex, but pain is an abstract and allows you to feel the negative of the positive. Negative is caused by the ego. You want to be free of that.*

P: Ray – sometimes people hurt us with their words or actions. Is there a solution or is it too complex?

R: *Pat – You have to realize that people come to this plane with many issues and when they behave in a certain way, it isn't necessarily about you. I can only recommend patience and understanding.*

*It is said that as humans, in our human form, we have many flaws and we all know it can be very difficult to work through these flaws. We think we're on the right track and we aren't. There are people with a lot on their plate, but that is no excuse. They must try to **love each person** completely and equally. Take care of each other. They need to step out of their enclave and realize **we are all one**. There is no "us" and "them." Otherwise, relationships don't work.*

September 8, 2015

P: Ray – In my heart I know you're with me and I can sense you. You turn on the lights and tell me in other ways that you are here, but I still miss you in the flesh.

R: **I know** I'll only be "gone" for a second. **You feel** it could be for a long time.

September 9, 2015

P: Raymond?? Raymond??

R: I'm here.

P: I love you so…
What am I supposed to be doing?

I know I need to be positive.
How am I supposed to stay positive?

R: *I will tell you a story about a woman and a man who were lost in the woods. One day, there was a woman and man who went for a walk in the woods. They thought they knew their way, but they didn't. The man decided just to go a little way to see if he could get help or find the right direction – the way out and the woman was left alone. She got scared and cried. She didn't want to be alone. Was her husband gone forever? No! Was he no longer in the woods? No! She just couldn't see him and so was lonely and afraid. You need to be brave – don't fear. I am here. The angels and so many others are looking out for you too. You are not alone even though you may feel this way. You have so much love coming your way. Yes, it is difficult and I know it takes getting used to, but just like the woman in the woods, waiting for her husband, it won't be long until they are together again.*

You must have faith. Inside, you know what I'm telling you is the truth. This story is for Liz also. I'm here. I'm in the forest with you. You just can't see me, but I'm right around the corner.

September 17, 2015

P: Ray – I love you. Liz and I know that to make better connections with you, we need to raise our vibration, but we're overwhelmed with sadness. How do we find joy within?

R: *Pat, I've searched for something to give you that reminds you of me so you will know I am always there for you. I know you need to feel safe and secure, protected and loved, before you can venture within to uncharted territory.*

I am with you – always with you
We are one and the same.
The joy will come from peace and contentment.

Sometimes peace just comes from being worn down and then being content with the small things.

P: Ray – this situation is not fun. You know that, right?

R: *I can imagine and would not want to be in it myself. Thank you for going through this. I know it must be very painful and has taken a lot of courage.*

P: I know you love us. I love you.

R: *I love you too.*

September 20, 2015

P: Ray – sometimes these days I feel very unloved.
R: *You are very well loved. It is a common mistake, though, not to feel loved if someone doesn't **do** something, people feel unloved. The solution is **within** – to open your heart and listen to your soul. Know that you are loved and your soul knows it.*
P: I love you *so* much!

September 21, 2015

P: Ray – how do I get through each day and the days to come?
R: *You are doing it. You are putting one foot in front of the other and you are moving forward. It may be excruciatingly painful now, but it will get easier. We will always be part of one another – just like your leg. I'm attached – we're one. I've told you I will be with you always and Pat, I keep telling you I will. Why would you ever doubt? You **know** me!! I have told you over and over my true feelings. You just need to integrate them, so you used to tell me. Look at yourself in the mirror and integrate this.*

September 26, 2015

P: Ray – anything you can tell me about Heaven?
R: *I am standing at the entrance with two ornate, beautiful doors, opening into a garden. The garden has many statues of old and young men and women. They are modern statues and beautifully done.*
P: How do people get around from one place to another?
R: *We are beams of light (Photos 4 and 5) but they also mimic methods on your plane. Why are there two planes of existence? The main reason is that there is a learning plane and a work plane. Yours is the*

> *learning plane although you would think it is the work plane. Ours is the work plane, although work is not stressful.*

P: Why do you work?

R: *We are all alive and our lives have purpose. We are fulfilling our life purpose and continue to follow it on your plane.*

P: Thank you. I enjoy hearing about where you are and where I will join you.

   I love you! Never forget that!

R: *As long as you never doubt mine.*

October 2, 2015

> R: *Pat – I am concerned about your health. Are you eating well and taking your vitamins as you should?*
>
> P: Not really
>
> R: *You need to*
>
> P: OK………………
>   I will……………..
>   Thank you………………
>   It's a little difficult to really care about yourself when you feel like you've lost a good portion of yourself – your essence anyway.
>
> R: *Pat – your essence is not lost. I am not your essence. I was part of your enhancement, but not the unique essence of who you are – your soul. That part – your light is only uniquely you and no one else has it. I think you need to re-evaluate. When you do, you'll see what I mean. I love you and try to help your light shine brighter as you did mine. You need to make your light shine brightly now. Not that you won't have help, because you will. I will still walk by your side. I will support and love you and help you to shine your light, just in a different way.*

P: But in a way I feel like my soul was ripped from me – I lost myself when you passed. I feel so weak, destroyed…drained, overwhelmed and exhausted.

R: *You must turn to your angels and guides. Leave your worries to me and the angels.*

  *Pat – please, we can all help. Ask for our help and then relax and let go. Let us all and the Universe work it out. It may not be on **your** time schedule and how **you** would have planned it, but it will be done for your highest good.*

P: Ray, thank you. I love you.

October 14, 2015

P: Raymond?? Raymond??

R: *Pat, you **know** I'm here. We have an appointment and I'm not going to miss this.* ☺

P: (*smiling*) I need information on how we can be better connected and how other people can be better connected to their loved ones on the Other Side.

R: *You were told to practice meditation. That's important. You were told to put out your intention. That is also important. You were told to breathe – the breath is important. It's just a matter of practice. Letting go and "being" is difficult for you, I know, and you are trying. Eat well, sleep, do Reiki, meditate – as you find more joy in your life, this will also help. You're doing great and don't give up on yourself for you are on the right track.*

October 16, 2015

Dear angels,
  May I please speak to my husband, Raymond?

P: Raymond??

R: *Pat – I wish you could see me so that you could see how proud I am of you and Liz and all the wonderful things you've done—all the hurtles you've overcome. You should be very proud of yourselves. I know I am, but I had every faith that you could do this.*

P: I love you.

R: *I know that you still think that I am separate from you, for that is the way you treat me even though I keep reminding you that we are one and only one. I hope that as time progresses, you will integrate this idea so that your pain will be lifted and the joy of us always being together as you always wanted comes to realization.*

Sweetheart, I love you and you cannot imagine the love I have felt from you or want to give to you. I thank you so much for continuing to send me your love and Liz, hers. It means a great deal to me and soon I hope you will be able to feel mine as well. I know we can do this because it is so easy.

October 19, 2015

P: Dearest Ray,

I want to let you know that I was able to sense your goodnight kisses last night. I was in bed. All the lights were off and so – it was what I call pitch black. Sometimes, when I would get into bed first, before you transitioned, and you would still need to shower, you would walk through the dark room – I couldn't see you and you would startle me by kissing me twice on the forehead as you passed through. The only-one-second warning I would have was feeling your energy rushing emphatically toward me, then…the kiss.

Last night, the lights were off. As I closed my eyes to settle in, all of a sudden I felt this profound energy zooming toward my forehead – quickly – twice. There was *no* mistaking it!

Finding Joy

It felt **exactly** the same as when you would approach me for the kisses. I **knew** it was you. It was wonderful! Thank you SO much! Love you, sweetie!

With infinite love, gratitude and joy for having been with you, being with you and having you love me…

Thank you.

And as always, I signed off by drawing a heart with two small hearts inside…

Chapter Sixteen

Acclimation

October 21, 2015

    P: Dear angels,
         Would you please help me to connect with my husband in spirit, Raymond?

         Raymond? Raymond?
    R: *Pat, I **love** you and I **am** with you. Are you feeling more comfortable with this idea now?*
    P: I'm beginning to. I'm trying hard because I know this is the way it is and will be for a while. I don't like it, but it is what it is.

October 22, 2015

Journal entry:
    Tonight, before writing, I was sitting alone in the living room watching TV. I started to think about Ray and decided to 'run my energy' – something learned in an intuitive class.
    I closed my eyes and instantly, in my mind's eye, I saw Ray dressed in a crisp, light colored oxford shirt and khaki colored work pants standing in what looked like a small classroom. What was playing in my mind's eye was very, very clear. It was as if I was watching a TV program or a film unfold. I was only looking at a portion of the room. Ray was standing with his arms up, like he

Acclimation

was teaching. I was looking at his right profile as he spoke to 3-4 people, seated at a rectangular work table. There was a blackboard or white board beside him. Ray was standing. The others were sitting, facing him like this:

When I wrote to him at night I asked:

P: Ray, I thought I saw you teaching in my mind's eye when I was upstairs. Are you teaching?
R: *I am and it is very exciting to do so on this side.*
P: I am so glad. What are you teaching?
R: *About building*
P: Were you teaching or are you just involved in building? It was hard to tell.
R: *A little of both.*
P: That makes me very happy!
R: *Well then, you can understand why I would want to be able to see you happy too. Would you want to look on at me and see me weeping? No, sweetie, right? You'd want to see me doing something I enjoy. And remember, it's only for a short time. It's like glancing at your child in their school room for a short period of time. During that short period, you'd like to see them engaged and happy.*
P: I will try, sweetie. I will try.

I love you very much. Your daughter also loves you *so, so* much, but I think you know that.
Thank you for everything!

Thank you, angels, for your help!

October 29, 2015

P: Ray?
R: *I am right by your side.*
P: Make sure you're always by my side! I love you!
R: *Pat – I want and need to tell you how much I love you and how important you were to me on the Earth plane and now. You are such a treasure.*
P: And you, to me.
R: *Right now we have the chance for a **beautiful** relationship. Let's go for it and see what we can do. We always loved adventures. What an adventure!!! What a journey! It's an incredible opportunity! Are you game?*
P: Is all of this **real,** Ray? Can this really happen?
R: *It can if you can believe it can. Do you want to try?*
P: Yes!! What do I do?
R: *You are doing a great job and I applaud you, so don't hesitate to keep going. You can do this. I will help. You will continue to write quickly and without hesitation. Your mind cannot interrupt us. Focus on what you need, so continue to meditate. This will bring excellent results.*
P: OK, sweetie
  I will say goodnight now.

Thank you as always to you and the angels. I love you.

Acclimation

Teaching Spanish, the students and I always discussed and celebrated the Day(s) of the Dead (October 31, November 1st and 2nd), honoring and joyfully remembering the souls of our departed loved ones. I would set up a memory table in the classroom, complete with flowers, candles and photos of the people my students and I wanted to remember. We would then place items on the table that were important to those special people. For about ten years, I had been celebrating this holiday at home, creating an additional memory table there. Now, I was setting the table to include Ray.

October 30, 2015

> R: Pat – I appreciate the memory table you made for me. It's beautiful and I am so thankful that I have two beautiful girls who love me so much and continue to love me even though I have transitioned. I think the idea of staying connected and continuing our relationship is wonderful. I'm speechless. You would agree. I don't want this to impede any other relationship, though, for you need people on your side too. We will be together for eternity…
> Please do not hesitate to ask me for help as I am more than willing and able. I can help you both with so many things…
> Don't think you have to be limited to writing to me in the evening – whenever you want. Wherever you are, I am there and will be happy to help you any way I can. You also have many other people over here who would like to be of assistance.
>
> I love you, Patricia.
>
> P: I love you with all my heart. Liz does too.

October 31, 2015

P: Dear angels,
May I please speak to Ray??

R: *Dearest Pat –*
If only I could hold you and you could feel the love I have for you – the love you are used to in your own language. Things would be so much easier. We are just speaking a slightly different language now, but one that is easily learned. You just have to be open and willing to practice. You are a linguist and this should be nothing for you. I will help. You have sought out help and continue to do so. That is great and I am right by your side.
I will continue to be there every step of the way.

Remember: Just a slightly different language, sweetheart.

I love you.

P: We are so grateful for your love, your light, your strength and support. I know I need to get used to it coming in a different way – in a different language, but it takes a little time.

R: *Pat – Listen to me…*
*Try to focus on the here and now, rather than the past – what you had, or on the future. Just focus on "now." Blind out the rest. If all you are thinking about is now and not comparing it to what you had or what could have been, then this is "all you know" and it should be easier. If all you've ever known of someone or something is **one way**, you deal with them in that way.*
Does this make it a little easier?

P: It does, I think…
I love you and I thank you and the angels.

Acclimation

When you were on this plane, you used to say you were on *my* journey and I was in more of the leadership role. I guess I am on *your* journey now. I think it is so funny, but I like the fact that you are the teacher. It's fun for me.

I love you and admire you.

Chapter Seventeen
Checking In

During the next two months, as we approached the one year marker, it seemed as though Ray was primarily using our journal time to review and assess the status quo. As a teacher, it was as if he needed and wanted to understand my comfort level with the ideas and lessons he had presented during the past nine months before moving forward.

He continued to reassure me constantly, telling me that he loved me and was always here – ready to comfort and take care of me. He reiterated that he could be in more than one place at a time and that I wasn't going to have to go through this part of the journey alone.

Any doubts or concerns I raised, he would immediately address. Any challenges I encountered, for whatever the reasons, he wanted me to know he was there to face them alongside me. He also gave me glimpses into his life, while sharing some of his newly acquired wisdom.

I continued to meditate and practice Reiki, as he had instructed. He would offer plenty of encouragement with his "great job, you're doing well! Keep up the good work!" In addition there was support from the candlelight in the spare room which had been on 24/7 since October 18th.

November 18, 2015

    P: Dear angels –
Would you please help me connect with my husband in spirit, Raymond?

        Raymond?

    R: Pat, I want to tell you a story about a man who loved his wife so much that he couldn't bear to part from her but he did and visits her every day in another form. He is so fortunate that she recognizes him as if he was alive to her in the same way as before. Do not, Patricia, think that you are the only lucky one for I am too. I love you and love being with you.

    P: Sweetheart, I love you so very much. It's true, isn't it, that our form may be different but the love energy cannot disappear and spirit to spirit we can connect.
It keeps me going.
You mean so much to me.

        Thank you so much.

November 19, 2015

    P: Raymond? Raymond? I love you…
    R: *(Whispering) I……….Love……………Youuuuu…………*
Do you know how much I love you?
    P: (Smiling) I do.
    R: *Pat – I wish you could understand that I'm here every second. I am not only here but elsewhere. I used to try to do that when I was on the Earth plane and watching two TV programs at once.* ☺
Do me a favor and continue to say, "Raymond is here and he loves me," every day.

> *Sometimes I don't think you've integrated it yet.*

P: You're right.

R: *You need to. It's true. There's no place I'd rather be than with you.*

P: I'm wondering if there's not a little fibbing going on here. ☺ Heaven is no comparison to me or here.

R: *I can't fib here, remember? :)*

P: I really knew that.

R: *So it has to be true.*

> *Oh – by the way, you were wondering if Bill and Dan are going to brunch on Sunday. They're telling me they **are** going. I will be joining you!*

P: Thank you, sweetie, for your love and support.

R: *Love **you**. Now, don't fret.*
We are one. We're together, not separate. The only thing that puts us in a state of separateness is you and your thoughts.

P: Hmmmm..........

R: *I know you'll think about that. I love you.*

P: I love you too.

November 21, 2015

P: Raymond…Raymond…

Sweetie, we had cake and your favorite food for your birthday today. We took pictures but we weren't sure you were there.

R: *Pat – I'm always there. I will not always show up in pictures though. But don't give up on taking them. You'll see me in blue light.*

(Note: I did not understand this reference to "blue light" until three years later, when I would be told by a psychic medium to look for deceased loved ones in photos where blue light appears). Photo 5

R: It was so nice of you to remember and have a birthday party for me. I see Donnie sent flowers and Bill and Dan remembered and said they'd celebrate my birthday tomorrow when you go to brunch. I'm glad you have them to watch over you for me. They are all very special men. They are a blessing and blessed. I watch over them too as do others so no harm will come to them. They have nothing to fear. Pat – take care of them, too, as they do you.
I love you and Liz very much. Always remember we are still a team and you are very important to me. Just as you don't want to be "without" me, I don't want to be "without" you and we will always be together.

P: I love you forever, sweetheart. ☺

On November 22, Bill, Dan, Liz and I met for brunch. And yes, as Ray had mentioned prior to my hearing from Bill and Dan, they *had* decided to go. I had made a reservation for four, just in case. When we arrived at the restaurant and were greeted by the receptionist, I gave her my last name. As she escorted us to our table, she turned to us and said, "Five for brunch." Puzzled, I shook my head and responded, "No." Dan quickly glanced at all of us, burst out laughing and shouted, "Yes! Ray is with us!" We all stared at each other for a moment, realized what was happening and laughed. Of course, I had forgotten! Ray had informed me the evening of the 19th that he would be going to brunch with us today! He was here!!

November 26, 2015

R: Patty…
P: Sweetie – felt like you were around us today. Some days I feel at peace and when I do, I feel it's because I sense you are with us – so I have nothing to worry about. I do wish I could sense and hear you even more clearly though.

R: *Pat, I think part of your problem is that you still doubt and please don't. You're doing great. Just go with it.*

P: What would you like me to know today?

R: *You **are** hearing me. Pat, in your heart of hearts you know you hear and sense me. Don't let others or yourself—because you are your own worst critic--dissuade you from believing it. You will get better and better as time goes on. Trust yourself. Believe it will happen and it will. I love you so and always will. I will be waiting for you.*

P: I love you sooo much!!!

November 28, 2015

Journal entry:

A well-respected local healing center was offering a holiday stress relief package whereby you would have an opportunity to sample three healing modalities – massage, Reiki and an intuitive reading at a reduced price. Thinking it sounded like a great opportunity, Liz and I decided to take advantage.

When I sat down with the intuitive reader, she didn't know anything about me. I was still wearing my wedding ring. She asked if my husband had passed, told me how it happened and said he wanted me to know that he hears me.

P: Raymond?? Raymond?

R: *Pat – I wish you could hear and see me the way I hear and see you. It would give you great comfort. I know it gives me comfort to see you and see all that you and Liz do.*

P: Ray – it almost seems unfair – it seems like we *need* to see you more than you need to see us, but we can't.

R: *Pat – it is time you realize that one never has to go far to understand that there is a reason for everything and there is definitely a reason for this...*

P: I guess I really know that in my heart.

    Ray – why did you have to leave when you did?
R: *Pat – you know that I never would have left you if it hadn't been my time, but it was, sweetie, and you will see why. You are blossoming into areas that you would not have gotten into had I stayed and the same with me and Liz.*
    We are all part of an infinite puzzle and a very important piece. What we do reverberates throughout the Universe and improves our life on Earth. Don't stress about what you need to do. Let it unfold. Ask God's help and where to go – where he wants you to go. You are doing well. Relax and enjoy. I love you, sweetheart.

November 29, 2015

P: Dear angels,
    May I please speak to Raymond?
    Raymond?
R: *Did you think I wasn't here?*
    I am. You should know better now than to doubt me. I would never not come when you call. I know I'm needed.
P: What would you like to share with me today?...
    Tell me a story! ☺
R: *Once aponce a time, there was a beautiful lady named Patricia, who doubted her talents and her strengths, but tried very hard to be aware of her weaknesses. The thing she needed to learn, though, was that it was very important to focus and concentrate on those strengths so that she could be stronger and realize all she could be.*
P: I would have liked to have been better for you.
R: *There you go again. You used to tell me you didn't want or expect me to be perfect because as humans no one is, but that is what you expect of yourself. Do you or are you upset with me?*
P: No.
R: *I'm not upset with you either. We all need to learn.*

P: But I'm not sure I've learned anything.
R: *It's all right. All is exactly as it should be and you are doing fine. Don't beat yourself up. Just allow yourself to be taken by God and let him make the plans and/or decisions instead of you. Discover his adventure – open yourself to his adventure – your journey. You'll be fine.*
P: I truly love you and am so grateful for you and your counsel.
R: *I love you.*

December 1, 2015

P: Raymond?? Raymond??
R: *Pat – I wonder what it would be like if you could see this Other Side for even just a few seconds. I wish you could get a glimpse into all the wonder to behold – the amazing things "people" can do. You would be floored! If only people could do the same on the Earth plane. What an incredible place it would be. But that space is for learning and this place is for doing.*
P: But Ray – why do there have to be *two* places? Why can't we just all be together in one place for eternity?
R: *Instead of asking that question, I would ask why it seems so important for us to learn in so many different ways? Each one of us has their own learning style – not everyone learns the same. For many the best way is with the seemingly harsh but very effective way on the Earth plane. People seem to learn faster here.*
P: Why can't people learn fast in Heaven?
R: *The temperament is different, the environment. It is not suitable for this type of learning.*
P: But there are people who say that you can continue to learn on your side.
R: *Yes, it's in a different way – different method. I wish I knew exactly how to explain, but I am new or feel new and it is difficult for me to fully comprehend exactly how things happen here.*

Checking In

There are different types of things you can learn on this side.

P: Are you still learning and, if so, couldn't you have learned these things here?

R: No, I reached a point and now needed to learn on this side. You, too, and Liz and everyone reach that point – just about everyone.

P: Can we learn on this side, but also learn from others on your side (while we are still here?)

R: Yes, of course, and there are people who can help with that – you are one of them. Liz, too.

P: I love you.

R: *(Whispering) I....................*
        Loveee...................
        Youuuuuu............................

Chapter Eighteen
Full Circle

Almost a year had passed since Ray's transition. December, with all its emotionally charged family "holidays," was now about to test our strength. Ray, Liz and I had absolutely treasured this time of year. In the upcoming weeks, Liz and I would experience Christmas Eve and Christmas day, New Year's Eve and New Year's Day as well as Liz's birthday, my birthday and Ray's and my wedding anniversary – all within Christmas week. But as we sat around the holiday table this year, it would be Liz, me, the holiday and the void of Ray's absence. Once we negotiated our way through all "the firsts," however, we knew we would definitely feel a sense of liberation and accomplishment. It was just wading through the dark water that was the challenge. With tears in my eyes, I smiled to myself. How I wish Ray was physically here to lead us through his absence.

Ever present in spirit, Ray continued to try to boost my confidence and self-esteem during journaling to give me the foundation and strength to carry on and move forward. Over and over again, he reassured me that there was nothing I could have done to make him or us happier or healthier and that no explanations were needed then or now. He would tell me he knew and knows now what's in my heart. He continued to emphasize that he loved me and was always here, "just in a different form…We are connected and part of each other forever," and that YES (for the millionth time) I was hearing him. He also asked me to repeat, as he had before, "Raymond is here and he loves me," 10x every morning and 10x every night to drive this reality home and to help dissipate any lingering doubts.

Meanwhile, the candlelight's bulb in the spare room had burned out. I couldn't figure out how to replace it (if indeed it could be replaced), so I substituted the old candle with a new one from the same set. I was hoping that Ray would turn the light on now, during the weeks leading up to Christmas, to help us through the difficult weeks ahead, but so far, nothing. There was a part of me, however, that toyed with the idea that maybe while Ray wanted me and us to enjoy the light (and knew I needed this now), the candle was actually only supposed to serve as 'training wheels.' What he really wanted was for me, in particular, to believe in his presence in other ways without constantly doubting. He wanted me *to believe* without necessarily having *to see*.

December 17, 2015

> R: Pat – remember the story I told you on the Earth plane about the mouse in our house that wouldn't be caught? He was cagey, and everything I tried, I couldn't catch that mouse but finally did. It's the same here, as I speak to you. I try everything I can to convince you I'm here, but you keep trying or maybe not trying but keep finding a way out.
> …You really have to trust and just believe inside what you know to be true. I can't help but think that if I were there in front of you, you might doubt as well.
>
> P: But you remember what it was like to be here, don't you or have you forgotten? We are brought up to believe what we see with our physical eyes. We try to believe other things – in other ways, but it takes a lot of work to convince ourselves – go against the tide, so we need traditional visual verification.

(Dear reader, I **really** wanted that candlelight.)

Still Beside You

Liz's birthday was the 23rd. We had asked my mom if she would be willing to come to our house to be with us and celebrate. She was more than happy to oblige. During the morning of the 22nd, I busied myself getting her room – the spare room, ready. The candlelight remained off.

We picked her up in the afternoon. We had fun socializing before and after dinner. Around 10:00 pm I walked into the spare room to talk for a few minutes and say good-night, when all of a sudden, the candlelight started pulsing!

Minutes later, I wrote to Ray…

December 22, 2015

> P: RAYMOND!! (My mouth and eyes wide open.)
> YOU TURNED ON THE LIGHT!!! (candlelight) Thank you
> SO much! I am *so* grateful!
> Liz will be too when she sees it!!
> R: Dear Pat –
> *I couldn't miss Liz's birthday. I told you I'd be there but knew that you and she would like evidence and Grandmama was crying. Tell her (Grandma) I love her and haven't forgotten her.*

Liz and I were SO excited!!

The next day, Liz's birthday, Liz, Mom and I went to the shore, where Mom grew up. Her hometown was a place that Liz, Ray and I dearly loved. We shopped and then had dinner at a small café. While we were having dinner, Ray's favorite song began to play in the background. We were thrilled! He really was there for Liz's birthday. He really was still taking care of us and doing a dynamite job. We were so grateful. All was as well as it could be.

My sister wanted Mom back home that night, and so we drove her home.

As we drove into our driveway and looked up at the spare room window, we noticed the candlelight still burning. We went straight to bed, getting ready for another emotional day.

December 24, 2015

For the past ten years or so, Ray, Liz and I had opened our Christmas gifts early Christmas morning. There were lovely traditions surrounding the opening of the gifts. This year, however, feeling it might be too painful to step into those traditions, we decided to open our gifts on Christmas Eve, before attending a Christmas Eve service at an unfamiliar church.

Liz and I sat in our living room that, in sharp contrast to years past, was sprinkled with just a couple of carefully placed Christmas decorations. There was no Christmas music this year or laughter, but there were smiles and gratitude as we opened a few very thoughtful gifts from friends, family and each other.

As our gift opening was drawing to a close, Liz quietly walked over to the hope chest where the presents had been laid out. She picked up a small, simply wrapped gift that had been sitting off in the corner, all by itself. Walking very slowly toward me, she placed the gift in my hands, all the while looking directly into my eyes. She murmured, "This is from Dad."

I choked. My heart fell. I froze for a moment while staring at the beautiful little package. When Ray was "alive," I had often expressed to both Liz and Ray that I had so many "things," I didn't necessarily need any more. Maybe practical gifts (of which Ray was a fan) or experiences would be better. As Liz handed me the gift she whispered, "Mom, I really had a strong feeling that Dad (after he passed) was telling me to buy this. I really felt that he was talking to me in the store. I told him you didn't want any more *things*, but it seemed as though he really wanted me to get this for you."

As she spoke, tears began to fill my eyes. "What could it be?"

Smirking, she then added, "So don't blame me!"

I smiled and unwrapped the gift. It was a *Pink Sleigh* box. For the longest time – before Liz was born and while she was growing up – every year as part of our Christmas tradition, we would journey to our favorite Christmas shop, The Pink Sleigh. Once there, we would each select a special ornament for that year's Christmas tree. We hadn't done so in a while, but Liz had taken a friend to the shop during the summer. While she was there, Liz said she really felt as though her father was 'talking' to her, telling her to buy this particular gift for me.

I slowly opened the box and brushing the pink tissue aside, a beautiful cranberry glass heart ornament came into view. I started to cry. I looked at Liz and said, "Did you know that your dad used to give me some sort of heart every year for Christmas?"

She said, "No…"

"Well, he did," my voice cracked as I spoke. "Sometimes it was an ornament for the tree, sometimes a ceramic heart or a little stone heart. He loved different types of stones." I put my head in my hands in disbelief that this could be happening. He *always* had a heart for me for Christmas. It was so like him not to forget.

December 25, 2015

> R: Pat – I had wanted to turn the light on for you today, but got very busy. I know how much you wanted to be sure I was with you on our first Christmas on slightly different sides of the veil. Janet was with you and seemed to be taking good care of you. I was happy.
>
> P: Liz and I were too.
>
> R: I think things went pretty well, yes? We were all watching you and trying to help whenever and wherever we could. We all love you and hope you feel our love today. We don't ever want you and Liz to feel alone.

December 26, 2015

P: Dearest Raymond –
How do I continue to live on this plane without you in the physical by my side?

R: *Would you rather have me in the physical for a short time OR in spirit for a long time?*

P: In spirit for a long time

R: *OK then…we are connected and communicating, loving. We can get through this…*

Pat – it is not for you to question the workings of God, but to believe that all is in its place and exactly as it should be. You and I (as all) are pieces of a puzzle fit perfectly together to create a beautiful whole. We each play our parts at different times and in different ways. But we are all together – our souls are all together in the end – in eternity – loving in eternity in a beautiful place – a place beyond description that God has created for us.

Pat, you will be fine. You will do OK. I am by your side loving and helping you. You need not worry about anything. I love you and Liz. I know you love me. There are many people on the Earth plane and here who love you and are wrapping you in that love every day. Allow yourself to be bathed in the essence every day. We are with you and you will see and be with us soon.

P: I love you *so* much.

December 27, 2015

P: Hi sweetie –
Tomorrow is my birthday and our wedding anniversary. We made it another year! You were just in a slightly different form this year. I love you so much! Please don't ever forget that!

R: Pat – I know you may not be able to totally understand everything I will say – but I love you even more than when I was on the Earth plane, sweetheart – which was a lot…
I know I'm not there in the physical with you, but I am with you always, watching you, speaking to you, protecting you and taking care of you. Don't dismiss any of that. If I could pick a thousand places to be, all one thousand places would be with you.

P: (Not understanding how he could speak so beautifully on the Other Side, I began to cry.)

Same for me, sweetie. Same for me.

R: Try not to cry. We **are** together. We **are** one. We **are** a part of each other's lives.
(Whispering) I……………………..
Loveee…………………….
Youuuu…………………….

P: I………………
Lovee…………………
Youuuuu……………………..

December 28, 2015

Early evening journal entry:

Today was my birthday and our wedding anniversary. I was anticipating a very difficult day, but it turned into as lovely a day as it could have been. Ray's sisters treated Liz and I to lunch at a beautiful restaurant for our birthdays. Their company, the lunch, and the atmosphere made it a wonderful day!

It was dusk as Liz drove the two of us home. It was very cold outside, but with the heat on in the car – like a fireplace –memories of lunch, Liz's company and the snow beginning to fall as we drove, I couldn't have asked for more. I told her so. Liz needed to stop for gas and so pulled into a convenience store gas station. Knowing how much I like Coca-Cola, but rarely drink it, she asked if maybe I would like one as a treat for my birthday/anniversary drive home. I was excited and said, "Yes."

When she returned to the car and handed me the Coke, she had a smile on her face and a glimmer in her eye. She climbed into the car and said, "Mom, so I went to the refrigerator inside to grab you a cold Coke. I started to grab one bottle, but then something strong told me to take the one *behind* it. When I pulled it out and started to give it to the cashier, I noticed that the bottle had a big message on the label." Liz handed me the bottle and instructed me to read it. In bold letters on the side of the label it declared, "Share a Coke with your **SOUL MATE.**" (And the word "soul mate" was in extra-large bold print.) Liz then continued with a smile…"Mom, from Dad… I went to the refrigerated case after my purchase to see if all the bottles had the same message, but they did not. This one is for you from Dad." I was stunned – my heart bursting with gratitude, disbelief and love for Liz and for Ray.

When we drove into our driveway and looked up at the spare room window, the candlelight, which had been off when we left, was on. Ray **never ever** missed my birthday or our anniversary. Thank you SO much Ray!

Late evening journal entry:

P: Raymond?? Raymond?
R: *Pat – I want to tell you how much I love you and how proud I am of you and Liz for handling – so well—all the things you've had to handle this year. You two are my little wonders and I love you both so much. I don't know if you realize how hard it is to be on this side watching you sometimes, but it is. I want you two to be happy and enjoying life but sometimes you are so sad. I know it is because you miss my presence. I apologize for this…you seem to be finding ways*

to experience some sort of enjoyment and I am glad. I love you both so much.

Pat and Liz – We still have plenty of time together so know this and integrate this. We are just "separate" as you would see it, for now. But we are one – remember that. My two beautiful girls, I love you and am always with you! (Pat – I look forward to the beautiful years in the future…Please remember that.)

Liz – Great job on Mom's presents!! You are one smart girl!

P: Raymond, we love you with all our hearts.
Happy Anniversary, Sweetheart!

And a final anniversary note:

Ray and I used to exchange wedding anniversary gifts with my sister, Em, and her husband. Ray had passed this year, but they had decided to give me something anyway. When I received their gift, a bit before Christmas, I placed it aside, thinking I wouldn't open it until the 28th. Then, on Christmas night, deciding that it might be too difficult to open on the actual anniversary date, I yielded.

The gift was the size of a jewelry box. As I unwrapped the present and removed the lids of the box inside, a jewelry box, indeed, came into view. Slowly lifting the top, a beautiful silver heart-shaped locket with two small hearts engraved on its face appeared. I gasped when I saw it. It was my drawing! It was just like the drawing I would sketch at the end of *every single* one of my nightly sessions with Ray!

I never told Emmy anything about my journaling with Ray or what I drew to sign off my sessions each night. I never told her about Liz and my session with Patrick Mathews and the "tattoo" Ray now had that mimicked the drawing. I never mentioned that on the April night after our session with Patrick, when I wrote to Ray, I told him that "I would like something similar to your tattoo and my sketch – maybe a piece of jewelry – a necklace? that connects us through this image." Or in July, when I wrote, "I want to get a locket…so I can have a visual of your being with us all the time" and he had responded, "Pat, I will see what I can do to find one for you. Your wish is my command."

On the evening of December 28th, I sent a thank you to my sister and her husband for the locket. In return, she responded saying,

"I (We) wanted to get you something for your anniversary. I started to go in one direction, but it didn't feel perfect. So I said, 'Come on, Ray, help me out please. What would be good for Patty this year?' And the thought came for the locket and the thought also came, 'Something to keep us close.' I told that to Mom. When I saw the two hearts, I knew it was right. It felt perfect."

December 29, 2015

    P: Dear Raymond –
    The locket that Emmy and Dan gave me – it was a heart with two little hearts engraved on its face – like your "tattoo." ☺ Emmy wouldn't have known what I draw each night to close our journaling session or what is on your arm now, on the Other Side, and yet she picked it out! You ***really*** are speaking to us for sure and we are understanding you! I love you **so much!!!**

    R: Dearest Patricia –
    *Pat – I've been telling you all along that we're communicating. You know it in your heart and you are doing a terrific job. We are always together, sweetheart – always together and never apart…Try not to think about missing me physically, but experiencing me to the fullest – the way I **am** and we **are**. Let us revel in the opportunity that we*

have been blessed with and share it with others so that they will see it can indeed be done.

The world, on your plane, places way too much emphasis on what can be seen rather than not seen. That old saying that what really matters is what can be seen by the heart is true. Spiritual things are not necessarily seen with the eyes but with the heart and Spirit—that's what matters. This is eternal and not transitory. This is the essence of all that is. Please try to integrate all of this. You actually know this already, you just need to have confidence to integrate and be very comfortable in that integration. I love you with all my heart.

P: I love **you** with all my heart.

As always, I signed off by drawing a big heart with two little hearts inside.

And so, dear reader, I had come full circle. Throughout the year, Ray had held my hand and with love and support, humor and wisdom, guided me through the darkness of grief. While it was difficult for my head to accept the reality of our connection, in my heart I knew the words breaking the silence of the night were not mine. Only *he* could speak in that very unique way.

The medium James Van Praagh has said that, "We are 80% spirit, so why wouldn't we be able to communicate with other spirits?"[3] I never would have thought it could happen to me. Yet it did. It **is** possible and I stand in awe.

Ray challenged me to alter my perception of reality, the Universe and how we relate to and/or experience one another. He truly was there for me, adorned with lights and feathers, hearts and songs. He was and is with me still. We are one and always will be, for love is the strongest bond there is.

---

3   Omega Institute, 9-11 Oct. 2015, Rhinebeck, New York.

CPSIA information can be obtained
at www.ICGtesting.com
Printed in the USA
LVHW071131150222
711189LV00017B/535